AIDS

Opposing Viewpoints®

OTHER BOOKS OF RELATED INTEREST

OPPOSING VIEWPOINTS SERIES

America Beyond 2001
American Values
America's Children
Biomedical Ethics
Chemical Dependency
Culture Wars
Death & Dying
Discrimination
Drug Abuse
Euthanasia
Genetic Engineering
Health and Fitness
Health Care in America
Homosexuality
Human Sexuality
Sexual Values
Suicide
Teenage Sexuality

CURRENT CONTROVERSIES SERIES

The Disabled
Ethics
Gay Rights
Hate Crimes

AT ISSUE SERIES

Physician-Assisted Suicide
The Spread of AIDS

AIDS

Opposing Viewpoints®

David L. Bender, *Publisher*
Bruno Leone, *Executive Editor*
Brenda Stalcup, *Managing Editor*
Scott Barbour, *Senior Editor*
Tamara L. Roleff, *Book Editor*
Charles P. Cozic, *Book Editor*

OPPOSING
VIEWPOINTS®
SERIES

Greenhaven Press, Inc., San Diego, California

Cover photo: PhotoDisc

Library of Congress Cataloging-in-Publication Data

AIDS : opposing viewpoints / Tamara L. Roleff, book editor, Charles P.
Cozic, book editor.
    p.   cm. — (Opposing viewpoints series)
    Includes bibliographical references and index.
    ISBN 1-56510-667-9 (alk. paper). — ISBN 1-56510-666-0
(pbk. : alk. paper)
    1. AIDS (Disease). 2. AIDS (Disease)—United States. I. Roleff,
Tamara L., 1959–   . II. Cozic, Charles P., 1957–   . III. Series:
Opposing viewpoints series (Unnumbered)
RA644.A25 1998
616.97'92—dc21   97-28424
                                                                       CIP

Greenhaven Press, Inc., P.O. Box 289009
San Diego, CA 92198-9009

"CONGRESS SHALL MAKE NO LAW...ABRIDGING THE FREEDOM OF SPEECH, OR OF THE PRESS."

First Amendment to the U.S. Constitution

The basic foundation of our democracy is the First Amendment guarantee of freedom of expression. The Opposing Viewpoints Series is dedicated to the concept of this basic freedom and the idea that it is more important to practice it than to enshrine it.

CONTENTS

WHY CONSIDER OPPOSING VIEWPOINTS?

> "The only way in which a human being can make some approach to knowing the whole of a subject is by hearing what can be said about it by persons of every variety of opinion and studying all modes in which it can be looked at by every character of mind. No wise man ever acquired his wisdom in any mode but this."
>
> John Stuart Mill

In our media-intensive culture it is not difficult to find differing opinions. Thousands of newspapers and magazines and dozens of radio and television talk shows resound with differing points of view. The difficulty lies in deciding which opinion to agree with and which "experts" seem the most credible. The more inundated we become with differing opinions and claims, the more essential it is to hone critical reading and thinking skills to evaluate these ideas. Opposing Viewpoints books address this problem directly by presenting stimulating debates that can be used to enhance and teach these skills. The varied opinions contained in each book examine many different aspects of a single issue. While examining these conveniently edited opposing views, readers can develop critical thinking skills such as the ability to compare and contrast authors' credibility, facts, argumentation styles, use of persuasive techniques, and other stylistic tools. In short, the Opposing Viewpoints Series is an ideal way to attain the higher-level thinking and reading skills so essential in a culture of diverse and contradictory opinions.

In addition to providing a tool for critical thinking, Opposing Viewpoints books challenge readers to question their own strongly held opinions and assumptions. Most people form their opinions on the basis of upbringing, peer pressure, and personal, cultural, or professional bias. By reading carefully balanced opposing views, readers must directly confront new ideas as well as the opinions of those with whom they disagree. This is not to simplistically argue that everyone who reads opposing views will—or should—change his or her opinion. Instead, the series enhances readers' understanding of their own views by encouraging confrontation with opposing ideas. Careful examination of others' views can lead to the readers' understanding of the logical inconsistencies in their own opinions, perspective on why they hold an opinion, and the consideration of the possibility that their opinion requires further evaluation.

EVALUATING OTHER OPINIONS

To ensure that this type of examination occurs, Opposing Viewpoints books present all types of opinions. Prominent spokespeople on different sides of each issue as well as well-known professionals from many disciplines challenge the reader. An additional goal of the series is to provide a forum for other, less known, or even unpopular viewpoints. The opinion of an ordinary person who has had to make the decision to cut off life support from a terminally ill relative, for example, may be just as valuable and provide just as much insight as a medical ethicist's professional opinion. The editors have two additional purposes in including these less known views. One, the editors encourage readers to respect others' opinions—even when not enhanced by professional credibility. It is only by reading or listening to and objectively evaluating others' ideas that one can determine whether they are worthy of consideration. Two, the inclusion of such viewpoints encourages the important critical thinking skill of objectively evaluating an author's credentials and bias. This evaluation will illuminate an author's reasons for taking a particular stance on an issue and will aid in readers' evaluation of the author's ideas.

As series editors of the Opposing Viewpoints Series, it is our hope that these books will give readers a deeper understanding of the issues debated and an appreciation of the complexity of even seemingly simple issues when good and honest people disagree. This awareness is particularly important in a democratic society such as ours in which people enter into public debate to determine the common good. Those with whom one disagrees should not be regarded as enemies but rather as people whose views deserve careful examination and may shed light on one's own.

Thomas Jefferson once said that "difference of opinion leads to inquiry, and inquiry to truth." Jefferson, a broadly educated man, argued that "if a nation expects to be ignorant and free . . . it expects what never was and never will be." As individuals and as a nation, it is imperative that we consider the opinions of others and examine them with skill and discernment. The Opposing Viewpoints Series is intended to help readers achieve this goal.

David L. Bender & Bruno Leone,
Series Editors

Greenhaven Press anthologies primarily consist of previously published material taken from a variety of sources, including periodicals, books, scholarly journals, newspapers, government documents, and position papers from private and public organizations. These original sources are often edited for length and to ensure their accessibility for a young adult audience. The anthology editors also change the original titles of these works in order to clearly present the main thesis of each viewpoint and to explicitly indicate the opinion presented in the viewpoint. These alterations are made in consideration of both the reading and comprehension levels of a young adult audience. Every effort is made to ensure that Greenhaven Press accurately reflects the original intent of the authors included in this anthology.

INTRODUCTION

"[The drop in AIDS-related deaths is] great news for all Americans living with AIDS and those who love them."
—Donna E. Shalala, February 27, 1997

"The AIDS epidemic is not over."
—Bill Clinton, February 27, 1997

In 1980 and 1981, doctors in Los Angeles and New York became alarmed about the possibility of a new disease when they noticed that some of their homosexual patients had contracted rare forms of cancer and pneumonia. The Centers for Disease Control and Prevention (CDC) identified the new disease—now known as acquired immunodeficiency syndrome (AIDS)—in June 1981. AIDS is believed to be caused by HIV, the human immunodeficiency virus, which is mainly transmitted in one of three ways: in semen during sexual intercourse, from mother to fetus during pregnancy or delivery, and by the use of a syringe infected with the virus. HIV invades a person's white blood cells and disables the body's immune system. The weakened immune system is unable to fight off diseases, including those that are otherwise not serious or deadly. These various illnesses, which are collectively labeled "AIDS," eventually result in death. However, recent advances in treatment have raised hopes that AIDS may no longer be fatal in every case.

The strain of HIV that is prevalent in North America is most easily transmitted during anal sex. For this reason, AIDS has disproportionately affected gay men. HIV has also spread rapidly among intravenous drug users, many of whom share needles. Furthermore, the virus can be readily transmitted from an HIV-positive woman to her child during pregnancy, during delivery when the baby may swallow fluid in the birth canal, or from breast milk.

From 1981 to 1996, between 750,000 and one million Americans have been diagnosed with HIV or AIDS. Of those, 362,000 have died. The number of AIDS-related deaths rose steadily each year until 1995. That year, an all-time high of 49,500 deaths was recorded by the CDC. However, the CDC is cautiously optimistic that U.S. deaths from the AIDS epidemic may have reached a plateau. In July 1997, the public health organization reported that the number of deaths nationwide for the first nine months of 1996 had dropped 19 percent from the same period in 1995—from 37,900 to 30,700. The decline in

AIDS deaths was seen in all racial and ethnic groups, according to the CDC. Whites experienced the greatest drop in deaths (28 percent) compared to blacks (10 percent) and Hispanics (16 percent).

The CDC's figures were consistent with the January 1997 announcement by New York City health officials that AIDS deaths had dropped by 30 percent for 1996. Canada reported a similar decline. According to the Laboratory Centre for Disease Control in Ottawa, the number of AIDS deaths in 1996 fell 20 to 30 percent from the average number of deaths during the previous three years.

The CDC also noted that while the incidence of AIDS (the rate of newly diagnosed AIDS cases) is still rising, it is increasing at a slower rate. In 1995, 62,200 people were diagnosed with AIDS, a 2 percent increase over new cases in 1994. In comparison, the growth rate of new cases was 5 percent from 1993 to 1994 and was in the double digits in the late 1980s and early 1990s.

Officials at the CDC attribute the decline in AIDS deaths to several factors: the growing use of drug combinations, or "cocktails," to fight the disease; the increased availability of AIDS health care; and effective AIDS prevention programs. AIDS experts are quick to note that the number of AIDS deaths had started dropping before the 1996 introduction of protease inhibitors, a new class of drugs that has been effective in fighting AIDS. Some believe that protease inhibitors will have a dramatic effect on lowering the AIDS death rate even further. "If protease inhibitors had been available for a full year, I think the reduction in deaths [in 1996] could have been 25 percent to 30 percent," asserts Jerome Groopman, the director of the Mapplethorpe Laboratory for AIDS Research at Beth-Israel Deaconess Hospital in Boston.

The CDC's report was encouraging for gay men—even though this group continues to make up the majority of AIDS cases. However, the news was not as good for women and blacks. Although the number of AIDS deaths declined 19 percent for all racial and ethnic categories, and 22 percent for men, it fell only 7 percent among women. Women now constitute 20 percent of all new AIDS cases, up from 7 percent in 1985. AIDS has become the third-leading cause of death among American women between the ages of twenty-five and forty-four; it is the leading cause of death among black women in that age group. Moreover, while the number of AIDS deaths fell 10 percent for blacks, the number of new AIDS cases among blacks rose at a higher rate than it did among whites. For the first time, blacks—who represent 12 percent of the U.S. population—made up a larger proportion of AIDS cases than whites: 41 percent versus 38 percent, compared to 24 percent black and 60 percent white in 1986. This disparity exists among children as well as adults. Of the 7,500 children below the age of thirteen who had AIDS in 1996, 58 percent were black. The CDC estimates that by the year 2000, blacks will make up more than half of all AIDS cases in the United States.

Although the incidence of new AIDS cases has dropped dramatically, health officials continue to express concern about society's ability to care for the increasing number of people who are living with AIDS. As people live longer with the deadly disease, they will create a larger demand for affordable health care. "The decline in deaths doesn't mean that the epidemic is going away," asserts Patricia Fleming, an epidemiologist with the CDC. "We will have a growing population of HIV-infected people [who] will need resources. . . . And to prevent that population from growing any further, we have got to prevent new infections." How to prevent the spread of AIDS is one of the issues examined in *AIDS: Opposing Viewpoints*, which contains the following chapters: How Serious Is the AIDS Epidemic? What Policies Should Be Adopted for HIV Testing? How Can the Spread of AIDS Be Prevented? How Can AIDS Be Treated? The authors in the following anthology present a wide range of opinions on the many controversies surrounding the prevention and treatment of this disease.

CHAPTER 1

HOW SERIOUS IS
THE AIDS EPIDEMIC?

CHAPTER PREFACE

HIV exists in the form of several different subtypes. In Africa, Asia, and other developing regions, subtypes A, C, D, and E predominate, primarily among heterosexuals, and are responsible for at least twenty million infections. In Europe and North America, B is the primary subtype; it is transmitted more easily among homosexuals and intravenous drug users than among heterosexuals.

In recent years, isolated cases of non-B HIV infection have been detected among heterosexuals in Europe and North America. Harvard AIDS Institute virologist Max Essex is one researcher who warns that because of this emergence of non-B HIV, and because subtypes C and E have been found to readily reproduce in heterosexuals, "we could face a much more significant epidemic among heterosexuals."

However, other experts disagree with Essex's warning that non-B subtypes could spark future HIV epidemics among heterosexuals in North America and Europe. According to Harold Jaffe, a research director at the Centers for Disease Control and Prevention (CDC), "E—watched in Belgium and Holland—hasn't acted differently than other subtypes. A new wave of heterosexual HIV transmission is not looming." The CDC maintains that it "does not believe that the introduction of other HIV subtypes into the United States would be the major determinants" of a heterosexual epidemic.

The potential threat posed by non-B HIV is just one of the variables researchers consider as they attempt to determine whether the AIDS crisis will improve or worsen. This and other issues are examined in the following chapter on the severity of the AIDS problem.

"Certain drug combinations could
reduce all evidence of [HIV]
replication to undetectable levels in
most patients."

COMBINATION DRUG TREATMENTS
MAY END THE AIDS CRISIS

John S. James

Treatments involving combinations of several drugs have significantly reduced HIV levels in many patients and have stopped further replication of the virus. In the following viewpoint, John S. James argues that with further research and progress, the use of drug combinations could eventually render HIV a treatable, nondeadly disease. He contends that it is conceivable that drug combination treatments might even eradicate HIV from infected individuals. James is the editor of the biweekly newsletter *AIDS Treatment News*, published in San Francisco.

As you read, consider the following questions:

1. In James's opinion, what is the "major problem" in treating HIV?
2. What is the emerging philosophy in HIV treatment, according to the author?
3. According to James, what practice should doctors and patients rethink?

From John S. James, "New Optimism on Controlling HIV Infection," *AIDS Treatment News*, June 21, 1996. Reprinted with permission.

Today there is more optimism among leading experts about the prospects for controlling HIV infection than at any previous time in the AIDS epidemic. This change (illustrated by a conference, "Can HIV Be Eradicated from an Infected Individual," June 12–13, 1996, in Washington, D.C., organized by the University of Amsterdam and the journal *Antiviral Therapy*—and by a major page-one article in the June 14, 1996, *Wall Street Journal*) does not reflect any single breakthrough, but rather a number of clinical research findings, which together are strengthening an approach to treatment strategy which began coming into public view in 1996. It is important to understand the limitations as well as the promise of this new approach.

SIGNS OF PROGRESS

In late January 1996, at the Third Conference on Retroviruses and Opportunistic Infections, early data from at least two small trials suggested that, under ideal conditions, certain drug combinations could reduce all evidence of viral replication to undetectable levels in most patients. And the proportion of patients achieving this success seemed to increase over time—the opposite of previous experience with anti-HIV drug treatments, which quickly reached a peak of viral suppression and then steadily lost effectiveness.

Today there is more data, and from different kinds of patients, suggesting that:

1) Under ideal conditions—meaning that treatment is started early, using certain antiviral drug combinations, in patients who are previously untreated (at least with all of the drugs in that combination), and with patients who can and do comply with the treatment regimen by using the drugs as directed—HIV replication in many patients can indeed be reduced to levels which are completely undetectable by any test known, for prolonged periods of time. No one knows how long this essentially complete shut-off of viral replication will last, . . . but in most of the patients who can achieve this suppression and who can continue using their treatments as directed, there seems to be no evidence yet that this antiviral success is coming to an end. Some people have been on treatment in the studies for well over a year.

2) If viral replication can be reduced to undetectable levels, patients do not progress to more serious disease, in the time frame seen so far. Again, no one knows how long this will last, since there is no long-time experience yet with patients whose viral load has been greatly suppressed by drugs.

Also, there are anecdotal reports of substantial improvements in ongoing AIDS-related symptoms in some of the patients. (There is no scientific data yet on this finding, as trials designed to address this question have not yet been run.)

The viral load in these patients is lower than that in long-term nonprogressors, who remain disease-free for many years, possibly indefinitely in some cases. But the number of persons who are naturally long-term nonprogressors (without treatment) is low, probably about five percent or less. By contrast, it appears that currently available drug treatments—when used under ideal conditions—can suppress all evidence of viral replication and disease progression in most patients, for an unknown period of time.

RESISTANCE TO DRUGS

3) The major problem in treating HIV has been that the virus develops resistance to all known drugs, causing treatments to lose effectiveness. It has long been known that the time required for resistant virus to develop varies greatly, depending on the drug. For example, with nevirapine (an experimental treatment recommended for approval by an FDA [Food and Drug Administration] advisory committee), high-level resistance occurs very quickly if the drug is used alone. But AZT resistance develops more slowly, and some patients can use that drug for years without it happening (although there is increasing concern about people being infected with virus which has already become resistant to AZT—and also concern that some AZT-resistant viruses may be more harmful than most nonresistant viruses, even aside from the problem of loss of effectiveness of AZT).

But now there are trials of antiviral drug combinations active enough to reduce viral replication to undetectable levels in many patients. And it is being learned that when viral replication is reduced to a low enough level, the development of drug resistance is greatly slowed, or possibly even stopped. The example of nevirapine shows how large this difference can be, since resistance develops rapidly if used as a single drug or a single addition to ongoing therapy. But in the right combinations, for patients previously untreated with any of those drugs, nevirapine appears to be useful for a long time.

"HIT HARD AND HIT EARLY"

4) Like almost all treatments for infectious diseases, this approach works best when treatment is started early—and when patients do not already have resistance to any of the drugs in the

combination they are starting (either from previous use of a drug in a dose which was not effective in shutting off viral replication, or by infection with virus which was already resistant). But there is no known reason why the same approach could not also work in advanced patients who have had many previous treatments, provided that some way could be found to reduce viral load to a low enough level. The problem is that it will be more difficult to find drug combinations which can do this for persons with more advanced HIV disease. This is why it is important to develop new and more powerful drugs, and better information about how to use them in combination, and about what treatments work best for different kinds of patients.

EARLY INTERVENTION

News that some scientists are seriously considering the possibility that new drug treatments might not only control, but cure AIDS has caused widespread excitement, and intense controversy. . . .

It may turn out to be easier to cure H.I.V. in the earliest stages of infection, when the immune system is relatively intact, than later after it has been severely damaged by AIDS. The immune system has some capacity to regenerate, but whether it can restore itself to normal after H.I.V. is eliminated is unknown.

Nevertheless, success with early-stage H.I.V. infection would encourage attempts to cure the many people who have been infected for years or who have developed AIDS.

Lawrence K. Altman, New York Times, July 16, 1996.

The emerging view of experts today is that what counts is getting the viral load very low and keeping it very low, regardless of how this is achieved—whether naturally in persons fortunate enough to be long-term nonprogressors, or by whatever antiviral combination works for the particular patient. The more advanced the illness, the higher the viral load is to start with, the more drug-resistant viruses the patient already has, and the more problems there are with continuing the drugs and using them as directed, the more difficult it will be to get the viral load low enough. To maximize potential benefit, the emerging treatment philosophy is "hit hard and hit early."

How low a viral load is low enough? No one knows for sure at this time. A viral load which is and remains below the limit of detection of the Hoffmann–La Roche Amplicor HIV-1 Monitor™ test—the only viral load test currently approved by the FDA—would seem to be a reasonable goal for now; for more information, see "HIV Viral Load Markers in Clinical Practice," published in *Nature Medicine*, June 1996. . . .

IS VIRAL ERADICATION POSSIBLE?

If viral replication can be essentially completely suppressed for a long time, is it possible that the virus remaining in the body would eventually die, meaning that HIV was eliminated and the person could stop taking the drugs and would be cured? This is conceivable, but at this time there is no evidence that this is possible. Eventually some people whose virus is now being completely suppressed by antiviral drugs will try going off the drugs, and then we should find out quickly whether or not the virus comes back. (Two patients who had undetectable viral load for two months and four months did interrupt therapy, and the virus returned; this was reported by Dr. Luc Perrin, of Geneva University Hospital, at the HIV Eradication conference mentioned above.)

Although there is no evidence today that it is possible to eradicate HIV in an infected person, what is new is that the question is now open. Until recently, all drug regimens had been observed to fail with time; therefore, there was no possibility that any amount of those treatments could eliminate the virus. Today, with better treatments, we do not know. But even if it turns out that HIV cannot be eradicated just by suppressing it completely enough for long enough, the new results would still suggest that for many patients viral activity can be stopped for a long time, and drug efficacy maintained, with combinations of currently available drugs.

Most of the drugs being used in the trials which appear to have largely shut off HIV replication in many patients are already widely available (in the U.S. and some other countries) by prescription or through expanded-access programs. The researchers running the trials have been unwilling to recommend particular combinations, since what counts is getting the viral load low enough, and the best drugs to use for this purpose will vary depending on the patient. Most of these regimens combine a protease inhibitor with at least two other antivirals. . . .

DIFFICULTIES WITH TREATMENT

One of the practical difficulties in implementing the "hit hard and hit early" strategy, as the [trial] results suggest, is that it means that people in early illness, who have no symptoms, are expected to begin long-term (possibly lifelong) therapy with combinations of at least three drugs. All these drugs can have side effects—and all are expensive, and often inconvenient to use (as most must be taken twice a day or more, some on an empty stomach, others with food, etc.). How many people will be able and willing to begin and stay on such multiple-drug treatment, when they feel completely healthy, and may understandably be inclined to leave well enough alone? How many will be able to pay for expensive treatment (especially when their insurers see that they appear entirely well)? The results seem to suggest that everyone who is HIV-positive should be on aggressive treatment with multiple antiviral drugs. But how realistic is this?

It seems to us that the widespread use of very early, very aggressive treatment will in practice usually wait until more evidence becomes available. Much more will be known later. And it is possible that persons with a naturally low viral load might need less aggressive treatment to achieve the suppression required. It is also possible that after a period of suppression, maintenance therapy might not need to be as aggressive as the initial therapy. But this is only speculation until more is known.

Meanwhile, physicians and patients should rethink the unfortunately common practice of beginning HIV treatment with AZT alone, or with other regimens not strong enough to suppress the virus sufficiently. This approach is likely to lead to resistant viruses, which might make future treatment more difficult than if the inadequate treatment had never been started at all.

| "We might end up with a super-epidemic that stymies even the strongest drugs."

COMBINATION DRUG TREATMENTS MAY WORSEN THE AIDS CRISIS

Gabriel Rotello

A main concern among AIDS researchers is that HIV could become resistant to new drugs designed to vanquish it. In the following viewpoint, Gabriel Rotello contends that it is highly likely that one or more strains of drug-resistant HIV will develop in the near future. Furthermore, he warns, touting the new drugs as a cure for AIDS may result in an increase in unsafe sex practices and a reduction in AIDS prevention efforts. Combined with drug-resistant HIV, these factors could fuel an uncontrollable AIDS epidemic, he argues. Rotello is the author of *Sexual Ecology: AIDS and the Destiny of Gay Men.*

As you read, consider the following questions:

1. What were the effects of antibiotics on syphilis and gonorrhea, according to Rotello?
2. According to the author, how much faster than original HIV does "super HIV" reproduce?
3. In Rotello's opinion, what group of patients would be the first victims of drug-resistant HIV?

In 1948, Thomas B. Turner, a bacteriologist from Johns Hopkins, gave a lecture about a new drug that was revolutionizing the treatment of venereal diseases. He called his lecture "Penicillin: Help or Hindrance?"

The "help" hardly needed explanation. Penicillin cured syphilis and gonorrhea, and many experts confidently predicted that these diseases would soon be eradicated forever.

But Dr. Turner knew that while both diseases are caused by bacteria, their transmission is caused by something else—human behavior, namely unprotected sex with multiple partners. He worried that if effective treatment was available, people would return to the risky behavior that spread the diseases, leading to unintended consequences. He was right.

THE SPREAD OF VENEREAL DISEASE

The number of cases of syphilis and gonorrhea declined in the years after Dr. Turner's lecture, but by 1965 the cases began to rise. Governments had virtually halted education programs, and the sexual revolution—spurred at least in part by a belief that venereal diseases were now curable—created new opportunities for both microbes to spread.

By the early 1980's, 2.5 million Americans were contracting gonorrhea every year, and syphilis ranked as the third most common infectious disease in the nation. Things came full circle when the casual use of antibiotics produced drug-resistant strains of gonorrhea that literally ate penicillin and rendered other antibiotics useless.

While antibiotics are indeed miracle drugs, which have saved millions of lives, in the end these treatments ultimately helped spread and strengthen both diseases.

I thought about Dr. Turner's warning often in July 1996, as researchers at the International AIDS Conference in Vancouver, British Columbia, announced the first glimmers of real hope in treating H.I.V. infection.

Studies indicate that when new drugs called protease inhibitors are used with other drugs, such as AZT and 3TC, which are commonly used for AIDS, they can virtually erase H.I.V. from the blood of many infected people.

A NIGHTMARISH SCENARIO

But this fantastic news, a triumph for medicine, is a mixed blessing for medical ecology. It could turn out that Dr. Turner's predictions for syphilis apply equally to H.I.V. Indeed, in one nightmarish scenario circulating among scientists and activists, society's reaction to the triple-combination therapy could render the AIDS epidemic more intractable than it already is.

That nightmare is based on three factors. One is that H.I.V. mutates more quickly than any other known virus, and strains have evolved that evade every drug, including protease inhibitors, and many drug combinations as well.

Second, the new combination therapies are extraordinarily expensive and difficult to take. Some drugs must be taken on an empty stomach several times a day with up to a quart of water. Others cause terrible side effects.

Yet, if people don't take the drugs correctly, the chance of developing resistance to the combination cocktail is greatly enhanced. And if they infect another person, that person may be drug-resistant from the start.

Sound improbable? The transmission of resistant strains "certainly happens with AZT," says Dr. John Leonard, who helped develop ritonavir, Abbott Laboratories' protease inhibitor, "and there's no reason this new class of compounds will be any different in that way."

"SUPER H.I.V." AND A RUTHLESS EPIDEMIC

Indeed, in the case of AZT, about 1 in 10 newly infected people have a virus that is resistant to the drug, even though they have never taken it. According to an article by Mike Barr in POZ magazine, some of these AZT-resistant viruses are a sort of "super H.I.V." that is considerably more deadly and reproduces up to five times as fast as the original H.I.V.

Combine the possibility of a multiple-drug-resistant H.I.V. with a third sobering fact. AIDS prevention efforts have faltered, especially in the most afflicted communities. AIDS is exploding in the third world and, in this country, among poor and minority people, especially women. The gay male population is undergoing a widely documented "second wave" of infections. If the potential for death hasn't been enough to compel people to practice safe sex, what might happen when that threat seems eased?

Here's the scenario. As the new drugs become the therapy of choice, many individuals may not be able to maintain the strict regimen and will develop multiple-drug-resistant H.I.V. At the same time, governments throughout the world may relax prevention efforts, while many people, rejoicing that the AIDS epidemic seems to be contained, drift back to a life style of unprotected sex with multiple partners. The drug-resistant strains could easily enter these newly reconstituted viral highways, and we might end up with a super-epidemic that stymies even the strongest drugs.

Nightmarish? Absolutely. Unlikely? Well, we could get lucky. Some drug-resistant strains might be less virulent or less infectious. It's also possible that widespread use of the treatment may lower people's ability to infect others and thus reduce the overall rate of transmission to very low levels. Treatment itself could become an effective form of prevention.

MORE RISK TAKING AND NEW AIDS CASES

Researchers such as Myron Cohen envision integrating HIV treatment into prevention efforts. "Our goal is not to say to an individual, 'We've stamped you noninfectious,'" Cohen explains. Instead, he hopes to ascertain "the concentration of HIV that's necessary to infect" on average. Public health authorities could then recommend that patients use drugs to suppress their virus below that level.

Aside from the ethical and legal tangles of such a strategy—would people with AIDS be pressured to take the drugs?—it might also backfire. David Cooper, a veteran HIV researcher, raised this specter in a speech at the closing ceremony [of the XI International Conference on AIDS]. "If infectivity is shown to be lower," he asked, "will this lead to . . . a surge of recidivism in sexual and injection practices?" In that case, less infectivity might be outweighed by more risk taking—and the epidemic could actually spread faster. Moreover, given the likelihood that drug-resistant strains of HIV will develop and spread, new cases of AIDS might be far more difficult to treat.

Mark Schoofs, *VillageVoice*, July 23, 1996.

But like global warming and other scary ecological scenarios, no one will know for certain what is happening until it already has. So it's wise to rely on past experience. And experience shows that drug-resistant H.I.V. has already appeared, and that in the last four decades other venereal diseases, far less wily than H.I.V., developed drug-resistant strains.

AVOIDING THE WORST

There are plenty of ways to try to prevent the worst-case scenario. One is to produce more effective drugs that are cheaper and easier to take. Pharmaceutical companies are already working on newer drugs. And activists will have to fight to make them cheaper.

Another is for governments to establish programs that provide physicians and patients using these drugs with intensive education. Some patients should also be monitored to make sure they take their medications as directed—just as the United States has already successfully done with tuberculosis patients.

Doctors should also consider whether they want to give this treatment to those who have demonstrated an inability to take medications consistently. This may seem cruel, but such patients would be the first victims if they developed drug-resistant H.I.V., which might place them beyond help when more effective, easier-to-take drugs are developed.

Ultimately, despite our best efforts, multiple-drug-resistant H.I.V. will almost certainly develop. So in the end, governments worldwide need to redouble their efforts to provide frank and effective AIDS prevention programs, especially focused on the communities most at risk.

Just as crucially, everyone must realize that in our interconnected world, safe sex is not just a temporary measure. It's an essential operating instruction on spaceship earth, at least until our viral fellow travelers have been decisively conquered. And that, I'm afraid, is light-years away.

> *"An expanded HIV epidemic could become established in North America or Europe before we realize it."*

An HIV Epidemic May Strike Heterosexuals in North America and Europe

Max Essex

In North America and Europe, heterosexual intercourse accounts for a small percentage of HIV infections. However, it is responsible for the majority of cases in Africa and Asia. In the following viewpoint, Max Essex maintains that the HIV subtypes that have caused heterosexual HIV epidemics in Africa and Asia have been detected in North America and Europe and could produce similar epidemics there. In particular, Essex contends, the United States' inadequate monitoring of HIV infection rates and HIV subtypes hinders efforts to detect and prevent the beginning of a heterosexual epidemic. Essex is the chairman of the Harvard AIDS Institute, a research and information organization in Boston.

As you read, consider the following questions:

1. How many HIV subtypes have been identified, according to Essex?
2. What is the significance of Langerhans' cells, according to the author?
3. According to Essex, which HIV subtype has most vaccine prototypes targeted?

From Max Essex, "Deciphering the Mysteries of Subtypes," *Harvard AIDS Review*, Spring/Summer 1996. Reprinted by permission of the Harvard AIDS Institute.

The HIV subtypes that sparked explosive heterosexual epidemics in Asia and Africa have now been detected among U.S. military personnel in San Diego, sex workers in Toronto, and hospital patients in Belgium. Should North America and Europe be preparing for a new wave of heterosexual transmission of HIV?

In 1992, techniques were developed that have since enabled the classification of ten HIV subtypes, designated A through J. The surface proteins of these viruses differ from one another by 20 to 30 percent—differences that may have significant ramifications for both the epidemic and our attempts to block transmission of the virus.

The five most common subtypes—those that have infected at least one million people—have been associated with different principal modes of transmission. Subtype B has primarily infected homosexual men and injection drug users, while subtypes A, C, D, and E have been linked to extensive heterosexual epidemics in Asia and Africa.

HIV subtypes also tend to be geographically clustered. Subtype B, for example, is prevalent in the United States and Western Europe. Subtypes A and D predominate in sub-Saharan Africa, while subtype C predominates in India and South Africa. Thailand has epidemics of both subtypes B and E.

The Mysteries of Subtypes

Two epidemiologic conundrums have eluded AIDS researchers for years. The first is why heterosexual intercourse has accounted for approximately 10 percent of HIV transmission in the United States and Western Europe to date, and yet more than 90 percent of HIV transmission in Asia and Africa.

The second mystery has centered around an HIV epidemic—later determined to be one of subtype B—among injection drug users in Thailand. Although this epidemic began in the mid-1980s, it subsequently plateaued at a relatively low level, with less than 100,000 people infected. Several years later, however, another HIV epidemic began to take hold in Thailand. Later determined to be an epidemic of subtype E, it has since exploded among heterosexuals, with up to a million people already infected. Most surprising, perhaps, is that subtype B—while present at relatively low levels in Thailand, India, and several African countries—has never caused heterosexual epidemics in those places.

Although differences in the rate of heterosexual transmission may also be due to factors such as sexual behavior and the presence of other sexually transmitted diseases, none of these considerations has yet adequately accounted for the widespread heterosexual epidemics in Asia and Africa. Investigators have begun to focus on how biologic characteristics of the individual subtypes might also play a role.

At the Harvard AIDS Institute, we have evaluated the way subtypes grow in different human cells to help elucidate these biologic characteristics. When we tested the five major HIV subtypes in our laboratories, we found that they all grow about equally well in blood lymphocytes. However, when we compared subtype E viruses from Thailand and subtype B viruses from the United States, we found that subtype E grew much more efficiently than subtype B in Langerhans' cells, which line the reproductive tracts of men and women.

Subtype B has an affinity for lymphocytes and monocytes, cells that HIV appears to target during male-to-male sexual intercourse and during injection drug use. And yet subtype E also appears to have a greater affinity for Langerhans' cells, which seem to be the target for the entry of the virus during vaginal intercourse.

NEW CASES OF AIDS IN THE UNITED STATES

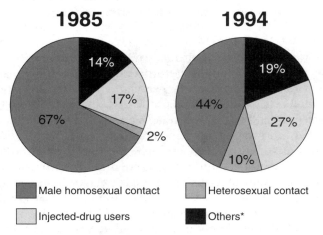

1985
- 14%
- 17%
- 67%
- 2%

1994
- 19%
- 27%
- 44%
- 10%

■ Male homosexual contact   ■ Heterosexual contact

□ Injected-drug users   ■ Others*

*Blood transfusions, other risk or no reported risk

Source: National Institutes of Health.

Our findings about these cellular affinities do not suggest that subtype B cannot be transmitted heterosexually—it obviously can and is throughout the United States and elsewhere. The point is that subtype B seems to be transmitted through vaginal intercourse far less efficiently than the subtypes that predominate in Asia and Africa. The enhanced efficiency of subtype E to attach to Langerhans' cells may help account for the explosive heterosexual spread of the epidemic in countries such as Thailand, while the heterosexual epidemic in the industrialized world has thus far remained at a comparatively low rate.

We believe that our findings about Langerhans' cells have important implications not only for understanding the dynamics of the worldwide epidemic, but also for AIDS vaccine development.

The fact that subtypes seem to have different affinities for attaching to different kinds of cells is critical to vaccine development, because vaccines seek to block those kinds of attachments. A single vaccine that protects against all subtypes may need to be developed, or a range of vaccines may need to be tailored to accommodate the cellular affinities of different subtypes. To date, most vaccine prototypes have targeted only subtype B. Yet to be fully effective worldwide, AIDS vaccines must protect against all subtypes and all modes of transmission.

KEEPING VIGILANT

We cannot afford to be complacent and assume that the non-E subtypes will not cause new heterosexual epidemics in the industrialized world in the future. At the same time, however, we should not interpret the recent appearance of these subtypes in North America and Europe as an indication that new HIV epidemics have already begun: All infectious agents must reach a certain level of saturation in a population before an epidemic becomes inevitable.

Yet an expanded HIV epidemic could become established in North America or Europe before we realize it. In the United States, there are several reasons why an epidemic of a new subtype could catch us unprepared. The policy of monitoring the epidemic through AIDS case surveillance rather than HIV incidence, for example, only tells us what infections occurred five to ten years ago, not what is happening now.

In addition, some populations at elevated risk of new HIV infections—such as adolescents with high rates of sexually transmitted diseases—are rarely monitored for HIV infection rates. Moreover, inexpensive tests that can distinguish between HIV subtypes are not yet available. Thus, routine blood screening cannot determine whether an HIV infection is due to subtype B or another subtype.

Such considerations should serve as a sobering reminder that new waves of the epidemic could take hold unless we increase our vigilance worldwide. We also cannot forget our responsibility to the populations already devastated by this epidemic. Finally, in our efforts to unlock all of the mysteries of HIV subtypes, we need to ensure that the AIDS vaccines we develop can protect all people throughout the world.

| "For the healthy heterosexual, AIDS
is truly a 'one-in-a-million' risk."

HIV DOES NOT THREATEN HETEROSEXUALS

Peter W. Plumley

Many researchers argue that the threat of HIV to heterosexuals is greatly exaggerated. In the following viewpoint, Peter W. Plumley agrees and contends that heterosexuals should not be overly concerned about the possibility of contracting HIV. He maintains that having multiple sexual partners does not increase a heterosexual's risk of HIV infection and that it is highly unlikely for a heterosexual to contract HIV during a one-night stand. Plumley, an independent consulting actuary in Chicago, is the chairman of the Society of Actuaries Non-Insurance HIV/AIDS Task Force.

As you read, consider the following questions:
1. What is a "healthy heterosexual," according to Plumley?
2. According to the author, what percentage of deaths among the 15–24 age group is attributed to AIDS?
3. In the author's opinion, how do warnings about AIDS interfere with sexual intimacy?

From Peter W. Plumley, "AIDS and the Healthy Heterosexual," http://www.aidsauthority.org/library/Plumley (cited 31 March 1997). Reprinted by permission of the author.

"AIDS"—its mere mention strikes fear into the hearts of millions. We hear that, while here in the United States it is primarily confined to homosexual men and IV [intravenous] drug users, it is increasing among heterosexuals. We are told that we should always practice "safe sex" in order to avoid HIV infection and the supposed inevitable resulting death from AIDS.

AIDS has been a serious problem for homosexual men who engage in high-risk anal sex and for intravenous drug users. But what about the "healthy heterosexual"—that is, the heterosexual who is in good health, does not have any sexually transmitted diseases (STDs) which might leave sores or lesions in the genital area, who does not generally engage in anal sex, and who is not sexually involved with the drug community or others at increased risk of HIV infection? Should the "healthy heterosexual" be concerned about the risk of contracting HIV from sexual activity, or is the risk too remote to worry about?

If you believe that, for the 85% to 90% of the population that are "healthy heterosexuals," the risk of AIDS is too remote to worry about, you're right. However, if you qualify as a "healthy heterosexual" but still are concerned about the risk of AIDS, read on. You'll learn about the present state of the AIDS epidemic (it's levelled off and appears to have begun to decline), whether having multiple sexual partners significantly increases your risk of HIV infection (it does not), whether condoms are really necessary for prevention of HIV infection (usually they are not), [and] whether AIDS education for heterosexuals is doing more harm than good (it probably is). . . .

THE PRESENT STATE OF THE AIDS EPIDEMIC

Acquired immune deficiency syndrome, known as AIDS, was first diagnosed in the early 1980s. A couple of years later, it was announced that AIDS was caused by a virus. This virus was called the human immunodeficiency virus, or HIV.

It is important to note that AIDS is not a disease, but rather a collection of previously known diseases which have in common the syndrome of a deficiency of the immune system. The definition of AIDS has been expanded three times—in 1985, 1987, and 1993—as it was determined that additional diseases supposedly were caused by HIV.

As of December 1994, a total of 441,528 AIDS cases had been reported to the Centers for Disease Control (CDC) since the epidemic began. Eighty-four percent of the adult/adolescent cases were attributed to either male homosexual contact or IV drug use. Seven percent were from heterosexual contact, with the majority of these being from contact with IV drug users. The remaining 9% were from hemophilia (1%), blood transfusions (2%) or unknown risks (6%). . . .

Unlikely Threats

Shouldn't young people be more concerned about AIDS?

Perhaps some should be; however, you really can't blame them for not worrying about AIDS. Only about 2% of deaths occurring at ages 15–24 are from AIDS, and less than half of these are attributed to heterosexual contact. Young people are far more likely to die from accidents, homicide or suicide—or even from cancer—than from AIDS. For them, the principal danger of unprotected sex is that it may create a life, not that it may cost one.

How likely is the healthy heterosexual to encounter an HIV-positive sexual partner?

Highly unlikely, assuming some reasonable discretion is used in choosing sexual partners. If you avoid those who seem likely to be at a higher risk for HIV (street prostitutes, obvious drug users, etc.), there are relatively few HIV-positive people out there. Depending on where you live, the probability of such an encounter might vary from one in 1000 to one in 5000 or less.

If by some unfortunate chance my sexual partner is HIV-positive, how likely is it that I will become infected from a "one-night stand"?

Again, highly unlikely. Statistical studies show that HIV is extremely difficult to transmit by penile-vaginal sex, particularly from a woman to a man. A heterosexual woman probably has an average risk of between one in 500 and one in 1000 of becoming infected from a sexual encounter with an HIV-positive man. A heterosexual man has even less of a risk if his female partner is infected. Moreover, these figures include both healthy and not-so-healthy people (i.e., those with other STDs, etc.). So if you are a "healthy heterosexual," your risk is extremely remote indeed. According to the experts, unless you have some special problem such as genital sores or lesions which might make you unusually susceptible to infection, HIV transmission from heterosexual contact generally requires repeated exposure to HIV, and therefore usually occurs between regular sexual partners, one of whom is HIV-positive, rather than from one-night stands.

So what is the risk to the healthy heterosexual of HIV-infection from the "one-night stand" with a seemingly healthy partner?

Virtually zero—usually less than one in a million. In fact, you're probably more at risk of being killed in a car accident on the way to the "no-tell motel" than you are of getting HIV infection once you arrive there.

Does having multiple sexual partners significantly increase the risk of HIV transmission?

Contrary to popular belief, it does not. It can be proven mathematically that the lower the efficiency of transmission, the less important the number of partners becomes. For the more easily transmitted STDs, the number of sexual partners makes a big difference. However, for HIV, if you are a healthy heterosexual the transmission efficiency is so low that the number of partners makes virtually no difference.

GOVERNMENT PROPAGANDA

The CDC's [Centers for Disease Control and Prevention] propaganda message is: Anyone could get AIDS! The fact of business is that for most heterosexuals, the risk of getting AIDS from a single act of sex is smaller than the risk of ever being struck by lightning.

Walter Williams, *Conservative Chronicle*, June 19, 1996.

Should I worry about whom my sexual partner has been with previously?

Not really, unless you have some reason to believe that he or she has had a regular sexual relationship with someone, such as a drug user, who was at increased risk of HIV infection. The more easily transmitted STDs travel from man-to-woman-to-man-to-woman, etc., and so one's prior sexual partners are important. However, because HIV is so difficult to transmit heterosexually, "tertiary" transmissions among healthy heterosexuals (where someone gets infected heterosexually from someone else who also became infected in the same manner) are extremely rare.

Can I get HIV infection from oral sex or shaking hands, kissing, etc.?

There are no proven instances of HIV transmission from oral sex or "casual contact." There have been some alleged instances, and there are those who warn about the theoretical possibility of it happening if someone engages in oral sex with an open cut or sore in his or her mouth. Even so, the risk is so remote that it probably isn't worth thinking about (unless your partner is believed to be HIV-positive, in which case some caution might be a good idea).

CONDOMS AND HARD HATS

We hear a lot of talk about the need for condoms. However, they are intrusive in the lovemaking process, and so most people don't like them. But are they really necessary for the healthy heterosexual?

Do you wear a hard hat all the time? No, of course not. They are worn only by such people as construction workers, those engaging in sports such as football and hockey, and some motorcyclists and bicyclists—in other words, people who are engaged in work or play involving a significantly increased risk of injury to the head.

Is this because for others there is no risk at all of getting hit on the head? Not at all. Many people have been hurt or killed from head injuries that might have been prevented if they had worn a hard hat while going about their daily lives.

Then why doesn't everyone wear a hard hat all day long? The answer is simple. It's because (1) for most people the risk of a head injury is very small ("one in a million," or less), and (2) a hard hat is inconvenient and uncomfortable to wear. So unless you are a construction worker or an athlete, you are willing to take this small risk in order to avoid the inconvenience and discomfort of a hard hat, even at a very small risk to your life.

The same can be said about condoms. Yes, it's theoretically possible that the failure to use a condom could cause you to become infected with HIV, just as it's possible that failure to wear a hard hat could turn out to be fatal. But do you really want to spend your life worrying about "one-in-a-million" risks that will almost surely never happen to you? . . .

THE DANGERS OF "CONDOMANIA"

Today we are in the midst of an epidemic of "condomania"—i.e., emphasis on the need to use condoms to prevent HIV transmission. While the AIDS epidemic is confined almost entirely to homosexual men, IV drug users and their regular sexual partners, "condomania" has permeated much of our society. It is a part of the larger epidemic of "AIDS paranoia." Because of AIDS paranoia, there have been tens of thousands of cases of discrimination against those known or even suspected of being HIV-positive. Dozens of laws have been passed to "protect" the public against HIV infection and AIDS. Many of those laws have been ill-advised and counterproductive.

"Condomania" has done little to prevent the transmission of HIV except among homosexual men. But has it done any harm?

Unfortunately, it probably has. First of all, there is some evidence that condoms can cause irritation, inflammation and other medical problems, particularly when used with Nonoxynol 9—the procedure recommended to ensure prevention of the transmission of HIV.

But the psychological impact is even more serious. Think of the harm we are doing. It is one thing to teach young people about sexual responsibility and to tell our daughters not to get pregnant until they are married and ready for children. But we are teaching children and adults alike that "intimacy means death." In the process, we are interfering with one of the most basic human desires—that of sexual intimacy—by telling millions of people, most of whom have little or no risk of HIV infection, that sex may kill them unless they "protect" themselves from their sexual partner, who may be carrying a deadly, and sexually transmittable, virus. We are telling them that they may die a horrible death unless they intrude on the lovemaking process by using some artificial means to prevent their body fluids from intermingling, even though for many that intermingling is an important part of the sexual experience. Surely for the healthy heterosexual the stress we are creating is doing more harm than the warnings are doing good. . . .

THE RISKS AND REWARDS OF LIFE

Do "healthy heterosexuals" get AIDS? There are a few heterosexuals without known risk factors who have been diagnosed with AIDS. But these are rare cases. Many more healthy heterosexuals have died because they weren't wearing a hard hat.

But healthy heterosexuals are not going to start wearing hard hats—nor should they lie awake worrying about AIDS. No matter how hard we try, we cannot avoid all risks in life—only some of the bigger ones. Even a life of celibacy doesn't totally protect against HIV infection—neither a hard hat or a condom would protect you against someone stabbing you with an HIV-infected needle while you were walking down the street.

This is not to suggest that we should not be sexually responsible. Both men and women have a responsibility to avoid unwanted pregnancies. We should be aware of the symptoms of STDs and get prompt treatment when such symptoms appear. (Fortunately, except for HIV, all STDs except herpes, which is not life-threatening, are curable with proper treatment.) We should always tell our prospective sexual partners of any transmittable diseases we have—even a common cold. And we should keep our own bodies healthy and drug-free and avoid sexual contact with those whose bodies are not equally healthy and drug-free.

But at the same time, we should not permit ourselves to become victims of AIDS paranoia. AIDS may be only one of a number of legitimate health concerns for the "not-so-healthy heterosexual." However, for the healthy heterosexual, AIDS is truly a "one-in-a-million" risk—the kind we take several times every day just going about our daily lives.

PERIODICAL BIBLIOGRAPHY

The following articles have been selected to supplement the diverse views presented in this chapter. Addresses are provided for periodicals not indexed in the Readers' Guide to Periodical Literature, the Alternative Press Index, the Social Sciences Index, or the Index to Legal Periodicals and Books.

John Gallagher — "Experts Agree: An AIDS Vaccine Is Doable," Advocate, February 18, 1997.

David Gilbert — "Holocaust in Progress: Underdevelopment Is Turning the HIV Spark into a Raging AIDS Fire," Toward Freedom, August 1996.

John S. James — "AIDS Survival: First Drop in Total Deaths in U.S.; Larger Drop in France," AIDS Treatment News, March 7,1997. Available from PO Box 411256, San Francisco, CA 94141.

J. Leland — "The End of AIDS?" Newsweek, December 2, 1996.

Jean-Yves Nau — "A Third World Epidemic," World Press Review, November 1996.

A. Purvis — "The Global Epidemic," Time, December 30, 1996–January 6, 1997.

Marc Schoofs — "The AIDS Epidemic Is Far from Over," Washington Post National Weekly Edition, December 23, 1996–January 5, 1997. Available from Reprints, 1150 15th St. NW, Washington, DC 20071.

Society — "Getting Younger," May/June 1996.

S. Sternberg — "Foreign HIV Surfaces in the Bronx," Science News, July 20, 1996.

Unesco Courier — Special issue on the global AIDS crisis, June 1995.

Bruce G. Weniger and Tim Brown — "The March of AIDS Through Asia," New England Journal of Medicine, August 1, 1996. Available from 1440 Main St., Waltham, MA 02154-0413.

Walter Williams — "Government Lied to Us About AIDS," Conservative Chronicle, June 19, 1996. Available from PO Box 37077, Boone, IA 50037-0077.

CHAPTER 2

WHAT POLICIES SHOULD BE ADOPTED FOR HIV TESTING?

Chapter Preface

Testing for the AIDS virus is a politically charged issue that juxtaposes the right to privacy against the safety of the public health. AIDS activists argue that due to the stigma associated with AIDS, all testing should be voluntary and confidential, while some public health workers maintain that testing should be mandatory for everyone who is at risk. Other proponents of mandatory testing go even further, demanding that accused rapists be added to the list of those who should be tested for HIV.

Proponents of mandatory testing for accused rapists contend that a woman has the right to know if she has been exposed to HIV by her rapist. They concede that HIV testing impinges on the rights of accused rapists, but insist the intrusion is justified. According to Susan Molinari, a former congresswoman from New York, the Constitution allows invasions of privacy when there is reasonable cause to suspect a crime has been committed and to protect the safety of the general public. Mandatory HIV testing of the accused rapist is necessary, she argues, so that the woman can know whether she needs to be tested herself and can take early medical measures to prolong her life. "Mandatory HIV-testing for accused rapists can provide information and desperately needed peace of mind for the rape victim," Molinari maintains.

Opponents of mandatory testing for accused rapists maintain that mandatory HIV testing would violate the accused's right to privacy and imply guilt. The right to be considered innocent until proven guilty is guaranteed by the U.S. Constitution, they assert, and mandatory testing contravenes that right. Furthermore, argues Bea Hanson of the New York City Gay and Lesbian Anti-Violence Project, the only way for a rape victim to know if she has contracted the AIDS virus is to be tested herself. Testing the accused will only reveal whether the accused has the virus, she declares, not whether the victim has been infected. The *Los Angeles Times* concurs, adding, "The confidentiality laws on AIDS and health status might serve as a barrier to knowing whether an alleged rapist has the HIV virus. They are no barrier at all to self-knowledge."

The questions of who should be tested, and whether that testing should be voluntary or mandatory, are among the issues debated by the authors in the following chapter.

"Would mandatory or routine testing bring an end to the [AIDS] epidemic? No one can know. But at the very least, lives would be saved."

ROUTINE TESTING WOULD CONTROL THE SPREAD OF AIDS

Helen Mathews Smith

Helen Mathews Smith is the former editor of MD magazine and has written numerous articles on AIDS. In the following viewpoint, Smith maintains that the best way to control any epidemic is through routine testing, tracking the disease, and warning those at risk. However, she notes, in order to safeguard individuals' privacy rights, the United States has not required routine mandatory testing for AIDS. She asserts that the current methods of tracking AIDS—voluntary testing and counseling—have not controlled the spread of the disease. The need to control the AIDS epidemic and save lives must take precedence over the right to privacy, Smith contends.

As you read, consider the following questions:

1. Who is experiencing the sharpest rate of increase in the number of AIDS cases, according to Smith?
2. What is the problem with anonymous testing, according to Stephen W. Nicholas, as cited by Smith?
3. In Arthur J. Ammann's opinion, as cited by the author, how is anonymous testing comparable to the Tuskegee syphilis experiment?

Excerpted from Helen Mathews Smith, "Are We Nuts?" *Women's Quarterly*, Autumn 1995. Reprinted by permission.

E ducation has not worked; neither have clean needles nor lec-
tures on "safe sex." We have condomized America, but . . .
the AIDS epidemic still rages out of control—not because of ignorance, but because narrow political interests have undermined
the standards and traditions of the officials responsible for the
nation's health.

A FAILED STRATEGY

For more than a decade, American public health officials have
pursued a failed strategy. They have ignored the central tenets of
plague control: routine testing, tracking the path of the disease,
and warnings to those at risk. Because HIV infection has been
given a unique legal and medical status, says Denver's director
of public health, Dr. Franklyn N. Judson, "we have gotten off
track" with a national strategy that is "irrational, erroneous,
and unethical."

From the very beginning of the crisis, public health officials
have seemed incapable of an appropriate response. Even though
it was clear by the early 1980s that gay bathhouses were a
deadly breeding ground for AIDS, Dr. Mervyn Silverman, the director of the San Francisco Department of Public Health, took
three years to decide whether to regulate or close down the
bathhouses. In an interview with Frances FitzGerald for her
book *Cities on a Hill*, Silverman said: "I may look as if I'm responding to political pressures, but what I'm responding to is
opposition from the gay community. . . . If gays start opposing
my decisions—if they start looking on me as a heavy father—
then the whole issue of AIDS gets lost."

And the last thing any public health official wants to do is
play the "heavy." In the early 1980s, Dr. David Axelrod, then-
commissioner of health for New York State, described efforts to
close bathhouses as "ridiculous." He also refused to classify AIDS
as a sexually transmitted disease. As a result, and with the support
of Governor Mario Cuomo, the testing and partner-notification
regulations that apply to syphilis and gonorrhea do not apply to
HIV infection in New York State.

Things haven't gotten much better in the intervening decade.
When a new wave of sex clubs opened in New York City in
1993, city health commissioner Margaret A. Hamburg suggested
that working with the clubs might be more helpful than shutting them down. "Our goal," said Hamburg, "is to reduce high
risk behavior through education."

This was certainly not the style of London's Dr. John Snow. In
1854, when Snow traced an outbreak of cholera to the Broad

Street pump, he didn't hold a consensus conference or ask local shopkeepers for permission to shut it down. The pump had to go, said Snow, because it was killing people, and city officials removed it. Snow, by the way, didn't know what caused cholera, and he certainly didn't have a cure for it—but he saved a great many lives. There are few public officials like Snow anymore.

THE EPIDEMIC SPREADS

The collapse of the nation's AIDS strategy is undebatable. The federal government has spent tens of millions of dollars on education, group counseling, and behavior-modification research. It has spawned a huge bureaucracy of AIDS social workers and neighborhood activists whose livelihood depends on what government publications describe as "culturally sensitive, community-based programs."

Two out of three middle and upper schools in the nation offer AIDS education courses, and the Centers for Disease Control and Prevention (CDC), the federal agency responsible for the public's health, publishes hundreds of pamphlets and brochures. The Gay Men's Health Crisis (GMHC), the largest AIDS activist group in the nation, with a budget of about $18 million a year, also has educational programs. None of these efforts has been able to stem a second tide of infection. Increased rates began showing up in the late 1980s, but it was not until 1995 that any media attention was given to the annual 2.5 percent increase in HIV infection among young gay men.

Since 1981, almost half-a-million cases of AIDS have been reported, and every year there are forty thousand new infections. Over sixty thousand women have been diagnosed with AIDS, and about half of the cases have been reported in just the last four years. The sharpest rate of increase is not among drug addicts, but among young black and Hispanic women infected through heterosexual sex.

In 1994, for the first time in the history of the epidemic, the ratio of young women to men shifted: more adolescent girls were infected than boys, and almost three-fourths did not know their partners were HIV-positive. Add high rates of youth alcoholism and drug abuse, and you have the next leading edge of the virus among all races.

What happened? Gay activist and writer Michelangelo Signorile gave one explanation in an essay in the *New York Times* in February 1995. Signorile made the point that out of a fear of "stigmatizing" AIDS-infected people, AIDS organizations have "placed most if not all of the onus on the HIV-negative person not to become infected." It is precisely this bias that is one of the root causes of the government's failure to contain the epidemic.

Widespread HIV testing was discouraged by public health officials to protect the civil rights of the infected, but unless those who are infected know their HIV status, they can neither protect their sexual partners nor get early treatment for themselves. After heated debate, and years of opposition from the ACLU [American Civil Liberties Union] and AIDS activists, New York State finally passed a law in 1995 permitting a rape victim to request an HIV test from the man convicted of raping her. Until then, a victim did not have the right to know whether her rapist was also her executioner. Testing continues to be characterized by public health officials as an individual choice—never an obligation. In spite of a horrifying infection rate of twelve percent for men and twenty percent for women in New York State prisons, HIV tests are still not required even of inmates.

THE YOUNGEST VICTIMS

I met two of the victims of America's failed war on AIDS at the Incarnation Children's Center in New York City, an eighteen-bed AIDS hospice and clinic in Harlem. Isabel Argueta is a small woman with short dark hair, olive skin, and an oval face. Beside her was her three-year-old son, Jonathan—a frail looking boy wearing chocolate-colored shorts that came down almost to his ankles.

When Jonathan was eight months old, he became deathly ill with pneumocystis carinii pneumonia (PCP), and it was only then that Argueta discovered that they were both HIV-positive. When she told Jonathan's father, he packed his bags, moved in with another woman, and then left for Central America where he is now dying of AIDS. Argueta says Jonathan's father was bisexual and involved with drugs, but she doesn't think he was ever tested for HIV. If he was, he never told her about it. She insists that neither before nor during her pregnancy was she asked to take an HIV test. Like the vast majority of infected women in America, Argueta did not find out she was sick until someone in her family became ill.

Jonathan, however, was not totally lost to government epidemiologists. On his birthday—July 29, 1992—he became a case number in an anonymous forty-four-state study to track the epidemic, organized and financed by the CDC. The founding director of the Incarnation Children's Center, Dr. Stephen W. Nicholas—a professor of pediatrics at the College of Physicians and Surgeons of Columbia University who helped care for

Jonathan—shakes his head in dismay. "Anonymous testing by the CDC," says Nicholas, "showed that since 1988 we had a major problem; we were not diagnosing AIDS until the child got sick."

THE RULES MUST BE CHANGED

If they are diagnosed at birth, adds Nicholas, "HIV babies can have longer, higher-quality lives. For over a decade, I have witnessed grief-stricken mothers and fathers learn of their own HIV infections as their baby lay dying in their arms from a preventable pneumonia. Those opposed to testing pregnant women and infants say the stress of knowing the truth is too much for them. Is there less stress in seeing your three-month-old child die? How much more stress would you like?"

In New York State, AIDS activists opposed testing for other reasons, adds Nicholas, "and as a result many women were discouraged from finding out if they were infected. The counseling message was, 'Get a test, but it may wreck your life.' Counseling and education failed. What we needed to get a handle on the epidemic was an effective public health system—we didn't have it."

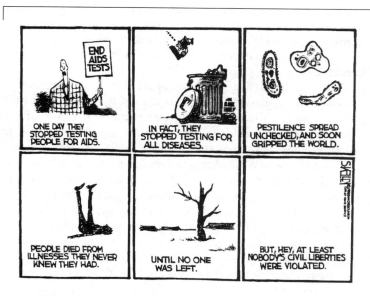

Steve Kelley. Reprinted with permission.

The director of research at the Pediatric AIDS Foundation in Novato, California, Dr. Arthur J. Ammann, says the problem is nationwide. "Once treatment for HIV-infected babies was available in the late 1980s, anonymous testing by the CDC should have been abandoned immediately, and all those infected identified." And when it was discovered in 1994 that the drug AZT could prevent the transmission of AIDS from an infected mother to her newborn there was, says Ammann, another reason "to change the rules." No infant, he adds, "would refuse a treatment capable of turning the risk of dying from a prolonged and painful disease into one of a normal life, but that is precisely the problem: Infants cannot be asked."

Ammann has compared the CDC's anonymous testing of infants to the notorious Tuskegee study that followed four hundred black Alabama sharecroppers infected with syphilis to study the disease's progression. Begun in the early 1930s, the Tuskegee "experiment," financed by the Public Health Service, should have been abandoned when penicillin became available in the 1940s. It was not—for more than a quarter-century—until someone stumbled across these unfortunate men in 1972. Ironically, it was the moral outrage of liberal academics that made the Tuskegee study famous. A research subject's right to informed consent was sacred, but the same groups that defended exploited sharecroppers are silent on the subject of AIDS research upon infants. The drugs are different, but the moral issue is the same.

How the System Failed

How did the public health system fail? An early preview of the coming crisis occurred at the Atlanta meeting held by the CDC in February 1987 to examine the future role of HIV testing. The agency's director, Dr. James Mason, said the meeting "was called to apply the best science, the best logic and wisdom to the task of controlling this unprecedented epidemic." The two-day conference—a cross between a university teach-in and a political convention—was attended by eight hundred people, including state and federal health officials, and the representatives of nineteen organizations, from the ACLU, the GMHC, and the National Gay and Lesbian Task Force, to the American Association of Physicians for Human Rights.

To track the path of the epidemic, the CDC proposed testing new groups, including pregnant women, marriage license applicants, and hospital patients. AIDS activists strongly opposed the new strategy. They argued that wider testing was unnecessary, expensive, and raised civil rights issues that would have to be resolved. They advocated instead more counseling and a mass-education campaign targeted to the general public. For teenagers, they recommended candid discussions of sex and condoms; for drug addicts, needle exchange programs. At the time, William Bennett, then-secretary of education, thought it was the wrong approach. Under certain circumstances, he said, mandatory testing might be needed, and kids may also need to hear about the "virtue of restraint." Bennett's remarks made a few headlines, but in Atlanta—where the important public health decisions were being made—no one was listening.

In the end, the medical establishment voted for individual rights. The prestigious Institute of Medicine, a committee of the National Academy of Sciences, declared that, "mandatory screening of at-risk individuals is not an ethically acceptable means for attempting to reduce the transmission of infection." But it was then-Surgeon General C. Everett Koop who settled the matter. From the nation's public health bully pulpit, Dr. Koop wrote: "Compulsory blood testing of individuals is not necessary. The procedure could be unmanageable and cost-prohibitive."

"The need for legislation to protect the rights of AIDS victims was endorsed by everyone present," wrote a New York Times reporter, "from dark-suited federal officials to jeans-clad advocates of homosexual rights."

A Radical Departure

An unexpected conclusion that was also a radical departure from public health principles. Exactly fifty years earlier, in 1937, President Franklin Roosevelt's surgeon general began a campaign against syphilis that advocated the opposite strategy. Faced by an appalling toll of death and deformity among infants with syphilis, Surgeon General Thomas Parran accused "public health officials and physicians of passivity in the face of misery." He organized an aggressive testing and partner notification system—before the discovery of penicillin—that brought the infant and adult epidemic under control.

Yet while Koop caved in to the activists, U.S. blood banks began testing for HIV infection in March 1985, and soon after the Department of Defense began testing all active duty personnel and new recruits. The procedures were neither unmanageable nor cost-prohibitive. The military did the test for three dollars, and blood banks dramatically reduced the number of transfusion-related infections. By the end of 1986, eight state health departments had begun successful programs of routine HIV testing and mandatory reporting. Two states that began HIV testing in 1986—Colorado and Minnesota—were and are today state models of disease control, common sense, and compassion.

Common sense, however, was no match for the rhetorical skills of the AIDS activists. The activists insisted that mandatory testing was a slippery slope toward detention camps. A few months after the conference in May 1987 the CDC offered two minor concessions to the traditions of epidemiology: It recommended that high-risk groups be "encouraged" to take the HIV test, but warned that individuals should not be tested unless they had received "appropriate counseling" and had given their consent. People have "a right to choose not to be tested" for HIV, said the CDC, and counseling should be "non-judgmental." Mandatory testing should be discouraged, continued the agency, because it was not the best use of money or personnel. As for pregnant women, those at risk were "encouraged" to take the test. . . .

New Recommendations

In July 1995, the CDC published [new] recommendations for the testing of pregnant women—returning to a position it briefly held in the winter of 1986. "Because of advances, particularly in the use of AZT to prevent newborn AIDS," the CDC guidelines recommended "routine HIV counseling and voluntary testing for all pregnant women." The phrase "voluntary testing" makes it clear that the agency is still stuck in the murky politics of the 1987 Atlanta meeting.

Some progress has been made, though: Instead of testing just high-risk women, the CDC now recommends that "all" pregnant women should be tested. . . . But the CDC still refuses to pose—let alone answer—the fundamental question: Can the nation continue to depend upon voluntary testing to bring this deadly epidemic under control? . . .

Dr. Sanford F. Kuvin, the vice chairman of the National Foundation for Infectious Diseases, says, "We have been betting on the wrong horse [since 1981]. One hundred thousand women of child-bearing age are infected, and clearly CDC voluntarism has failed. All pregnant women should be mandatorily tested for HIV, have mandatory counseling, and—if positive—be offered AZT during pregnancy."

Would mandatory or routine testing bring an end to the epidemic? No one can know. But at the very least, lives would be saved, and public health policy would no longer represent a retreat from common decency and sense. The nation has a moral duty to care for those who are infected, but the infected also have a responsibility to those with whom they share their lives—and bodies. Public health officials once enforced that responsibility. They need to do so again.

"Counseling and voluntary testing are more effective than forced testing because they encourage women to receive ongoing medical care for themselves and their babies."

MANDATORY TESTING OF PREGNANT WOMEN AND INFANTS WOULD NOT REDUCE THE SPREAD OF AIDS

American Civil Liberties Union

In the following viewpoint, the American Civil Liberties Union (ACLU) contends that mandatory HIV testing of pregnant women and newborn babies would deter many women from seeking health care for themselves and their infants. Furthermore, the ACLU argues, mandatory testing of these individuals would violate their constitutional right to privacy. The organization maintains that HIV counseling and voluntary testing provide a better way of protecting the health of pregnant women and newborns. The ACLU is a national organization that works to defend civil rights guaranteed by the U.S. Constitution.

As you read, consider the following questions:
1. What does an HIV test of a newborn baby actually indicate, according to the ACLU?
2. How can the risk of maternal-infant transmission of HIV be reduced, according to the organization?
3. In the ACLU's opinion, how might mandatory HIV testing affect low-income women?

The American Civil Liberties Union opposes mandatory, non-consensual HIV testing of pregnant women and newborns. We all have the right, protected by the Constitution, to be free of unnecessary government control. To take any compulsory medical action—such as forced HIV testing—the government must prove that there is no less intrusive means of achieving its goal of promoting public health. In the case of pregnant women and newborns, the facts do not justify mandatory HIV testing but rather show that counseling and voluntary testing is a less intrusive way of promoting health. Indeed, counseling and voluntary testing are more effective than forced testing because they encourage women to receive ongoing medical care for themselves and their babies, instead of driving them away from health care services. The Centers for Disease Control and Prevention (CDC), the government's own medical experts, have recommended counseling and voluntary testing, as opposed to mandatory testing. Opponents of testing without consent also include the American Academy of Pediatrics (AAP), the American College of Obstetrics & Gynecology (ACOG) and the March of Dimes.

TESTING NEWBORNS FOR HIV

The CDC currently tests unidentified blood samples of newborns in order to better understand the nature and extent of HIV in this country. Because the CDC testing is done not for the purpose of diagnosis but for statistical tracking, the samples are not name-labelled, nor are they collected or tested in the manner in which a sample would be if it were to be tested for diagnostic purposes. The CDC's mission is not to provide diagnostic laboratory testing, and the CDC may very well consider a testing program that had to be redesigned to accommodate diagnostic as well as epidemiological uses to be excessively compromised. Thus, "unblinding" of the CDC study could result in no universal newborn HIV screening for any purpose.

The results of HIV tests of newborns indicate not whether the newborn is HIV-infected, but whether maternal HIV antibodies are present. If a newborn tests positive, we learn that the mother has HIV and that the odds are roughly one in four that the infant itself is HIV positive. Unfortunately, there is no post-birth treatment at this time to reduce these odds—AZT or other antiretroviral drugs do not prevent sero-conversion in the infant. The primary treatment is antibiotics administered prophylactically several times a day to ward off PCP (an AIDS-induced pneumonia that is particularly virulent in infants) and to wait for a period of several weeks, after which it is possible to determine an infant's own HIV status by further laboratory tests.

REDUCING THE RISK OF PRENATAL HIV TRANSMISSION

However, before and during birth, steps can be taken to reduce the risk of maternal-infant transmission. One study suggests that AZT given after the fourteenth week of pregnancy, continued during delivery and given to the new infant for the first six weeks of life can reduce the risk of infection to the infant by as much as two-thirds, from approximately 25% (one in four) to 8% (one in twelve).

Any opportunity for prevention of in utero HIV infection makes bringing women into prenatal care crucial. Not only does prenatal care decrease the risk of prematurity with its markedly increased mortality, it also provides the opportunity for the woman to learn about her HIV status and the benefits and risks of AZT treatment as a prevention for infecting her infant. Additionally, knowledge of maternal HIV status before birth makes possible a decision to deliver by caesarian section, which is believed to further reduce the risk of infecting the infant. Another reason for early detection of HIV infection in pregnancy is to advise the infected mother not to breast-feed. Although this has not been a major problem in the United States because so few women at higher risk of HIV infection breast-feed, proponents of mandatory HIV testing of newborns cite protection against infection from breast-feeding as one of the benefits of such testing. They ignore the critical fact that breast-feeding must begin shortly after birth, several days before existing tests can be completed to determine the presence of maternal HIV antibodies. In fact, colostrum, the breast secretion during the first early days after birth, may pose a greater threat of infection to the infant than milk produced thereafter. These facts provide further support for the importance of prenatal care, including counseling and voluntary testing, as opposed to mandatory newborn testing.

VOLUNTARY TESTING IS MORE EFFECTIVE

As the CDC has confirmed, counseling and voluntary testing of pregnant women for HIV is more effective than mandatory testing. Mandatory testing of pregnant women and newborns would have detrimental public health consequences, most significantly by deterring women, especially low income women, from seeking prenatal care at all. Whenever mandatory testing has been imposed people have been frightened away. For example, during the two years that the state of Illinois required HIV-antibody testing of people seeking marriage licenses, approximately 40,000 people left the state to get married elsewhere.

By frightening women away from health care providers both during and after pregnancy, some HIV-infected children will neither be identified nor treated. Mandatory testing of a recalcitrant patient will accomplish only ascertainment of HIV status—it does not get either the mother or her child into treatment. Any type of effective medical treatment for children requires the participation and cooperation of their caretakers. Proper management of chronic, infectious, incurable disease in a family requires a tremendous amount of effort—and mother-and-doctor teamwork—over time, particularly when both mother and child are afflicted. Medicines must be given regularly, procedures must be developed and followed, regular doctor's visits are critical. Without trust there is rarely compliance, especially when a woman is confronting not only the possibility that her child has an incurable disease but the certainty that she does as well.

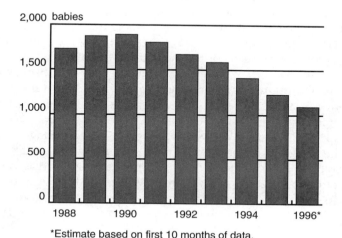

DECLINING NUMBERS OF HIV-POSITIVE NEWBORNS

In the 1990s, the number of infants born in New York who test positive for HIV has declined. Of these newborns, one in four will actually become infected with the virus.

*Estimate based on first 10 months of data.

New York State Department of Health

Another fact which would drive women away from health care providers who forcibly test them or their children is that these women are susceptible to the same kinds of discrimination faced by others if it becomes known that they are infected with HIV. The possible losses of custody of their children, of their jobs, health insurance, apartments, and other harms, including the risk of broader disclosure and dissemination of their HIV status, are all very real concerns. In addition, many African-American and Latina women may fear mandatory testing and the disclosure of the results based on past histories of discrimination and also due to past negative experiences with health care providers.

INFORMED CONSENT

In other situations where there is undisputed medical value in learning test results, the sensitivity of the issues involved and the nature of the personal decisions they engender has led to a recognition that such tests should be done only when the patient consents. For example, amniocentesis testing for chromosomal abnormalities and hereditary diseases is recommended for pregnant women over age 35—but it is not mandated by law. Screening for Downs' syndrome and sickle cell diseases are treated similarly. While syphilis testing for pregnant women is mandatory, syphilis can be safely and effectively cured and mandatory syphilis testing does not drive women away from health care providers.

Currently there is no requirement that pregnant women be routinely educated about HIV and possible treatments to reduce the risk of infecting their babies, or given the opportunity to be tested for HIV. Yet such counseling at the beginning of pregnancy makes the most sense in terms of the parent's decision-making ability about health consequences for the child. Routine noncoercive counseling regarding the benefits and burdens of testing and treatment ensures that rational choices are made by the prospective parents at the most appropriate time. Linking testing to the provision of services has been shown to increase the rate of voluntary consent for testing. Experience indicates that under these circumstances most women will probably agree to be tested, and they can then make informed decisions about the use of AZT, antibiotics and other treatments while pregnant or after birth. For example, at Harlem Hospital in New York City, over 90% of counseled women consent to testing. Similar proportions have been reported at Johns Hopkins Hospital in Baltimore, Maryland, at Grady Hospital in Atlanta, Georgia and elsewhere. If, after counseling, women do not get tested for HIV, they will have the knowledge to make reasoned choices about breast-feeding, caesarean sections and termination of the pregnancy.

A non-coercive health care environment, ongoing care, and access to services are what will bring women and children to health care services—mandatory HIV testing will drive them away.

MANDATORY TESTING IS UNCONSTITUTIONAL

Counseling and voluntary HIV testing are a constitutionally required, less-intrusive alternative to mandatory testing of pregnant women and newborns. Non-consensual testing implicates a broad range of constitutional protections. Pregnant women and mothers of newborns, like everyone else in this country, have the right to decision making about their own bodies; the right to control over medical information; the right to be free of unreasonable searches and seizures by the government; and the right to direct the course of their medical treatment and the medical treatment of their children. They also have the right to equal protection of the law, which is called into question by testing provisions which single out pregnant women, but not men considering having children, as well as by disproportionately affecting women of color.

When these rights are intruded upon, the Constitution requires that the government act in the least intrusive way that will further its goal. The goal of HIV-testing programs is the promotion of health. Counseling and voluntary testing are far less intrusive measures than mandatory, non-consensual testing, and experience strongly indicates that counseling and voluntary testing will more effectively further the goal of promoting health than forced testing would.

More than a decade into the AIDS epidemic in this country we have learned that the spread of HIV is most effectively controlled by voluntary, rather than coercive, measures. If we are truly concerned with the health of women and children then this principle must not be forgotten. To advance the health of women and children and to comply with the constitutional imperative of least intrusive alternatives, counseling and voluntary testing and treatment programs for pregnant women and newborns should be implemented to encourage them to receive ongoing medical care.

"The accessibility and anonymity of
the [home HIV] test will encourage
more people to be tested."

HOME HIV TESTS WILL REDUCE THE SPREAD OF AIDS

William O. Fabbri

The Food and Drug Administration approved the sale and use of home test kits for HIV in July 1996. In the following viewpoint, which was written before the kits were approved, William O. Fabbri argues that permitting the sale and use of kits to test HIV status at home would prompt more people to find out their HIV status. Fabbri asserts that many people who are unwilling or unable to go to an HIV testing clinic would welcome the option of using an anonymous at-home test. Knowing one's HIV status is vitally important, he maintains, in order to reduce the risk of exposing others to HIV. Furthermore, Fabbri contends, the earlier testing for HIV is done, the sooner treatments for HIV can begin, thus lengthening the patient's life span or improving the patient's quality of life. Fabbri is a lawyer in Boston.

As you read, consider the following questions:

1. According to Fabbri, what percentage of those infected with HIV have not been tested?
2. What is the author's response to criticism about the effectiveness of telephone counseling?
3. In what ways are concerns about abuse of home HIV tests inflated, according to Fabbri?

Excerpted from William O. Fabbri, "Home HIV Testing and Conflicts with State HIV Testing Regulations," *American Journal of Law & Medicine*, vol. 21 (1995), pp. 419-44. Reprinted with the permission of the author and of the American Society of Law, Medicine, and Ethics and Boston University Law School. (Some footnotes have been omitted here.)

As of December 1995, the number of AIDS-related deaths in the United States has reached 311,000 and at least one million more Americans are infected with HIV. Of those one million or more infected, many spread the virus unknowingly as approximately forty percent of those infected have never been tested. More than eighty-five percent of the U.S. population has never been tested for HIV. No cure or vaccine for HIV currently exists.

The federal and state governments have set up a patchwork of free and confidential HIV testing at local clinics. States have enacted a variety of legislation concerning HIV testing and test results. Most states have enacted statutes that require informed consent for an HIV test to be conducted. All states require the reporting of AIDS cases, and many also require the reporting of HIV-positive status to state public health departments. Furthermore, many states mandate certain requirements for HIV counseling. . . .

In January 1986, the FDA [Food and Drug Administration] received its first notification of a manufacturer's intent to market a home HIV test. The FDA rejected home HIV tests in 1988. Support for the test increased within the FDA and in 1994, the FDA's Blood Products Advisory Panel suggested that manufacturers undertake premarket studies of the home test. Finally, the FDA issued new guidelines in February 1995, asserting that home HIV tests may be approvable. [The FDA approved home tests for HIV in July 1996.]

The home test model the FDA is currently considering, called Confide, is made by Direct Access Diagnostics, a division of Johnson & Johnson. The test kit includes instructions and a pamphlet with AIDS information in both English and Spanish, a lancet, special paper for the blood sample that is marked with an individual identification code, and a return envelope.

The user of this test pricks his or her finger and places three drops of blood on the special paper. The sample is then mailed to a laboratory. In approximately one week, the user calls to receive the test results using the identification code. If the results are negative, a recorded message provides the information along with general HIV prevention advice. If the results are positive, a trained counselor comes on the phone and provides counseling and information concerning possible retesting, treatment, and the location of medical, legal, and counseling services. Follow-up counseling is available for a specified number of sessions. . . .

Initial opposition to the test has weakened, and currently there is strong general support for the home HIV test. Approval of the home test appears probable according to FDA chairman

David Kessler, and as evidenced by the new guidelines. However, despite this strong support, several arguments against and concerns regarding home HIV tests have been raised by many clinics and gay and lesbian rights groups, among others.

Some of the earlier concerns have faded away. For example, when the first home test was prepared for FDA consideration, the accuracy of the test was a concern. The test now under consideration uses the same testing methods on the sample, and matches the accuracy of HIV tests performed by doctors or clinics. After examining and analyzing the arguments, I believe that the home HIV test is worthy of FDA approval.

THE IMPORTANCE OF HOME HIV TESTING

Proponents of the home HIV test argue that the accessibility and anonymity of the test will encourage more people to be tested. Surveys reveal that twenty-nine percent of adults would likely use a home test—three times the number of people who indicated they would use current options. This number increases to forty-two percent when limited to those defined at risk for infection.

Forty percent of those infected with HIV have not been tested. Furthermore, information is currently the only tool available in the battle against AIDS. There is no cure or vaccine, nor does there appear to be hope for one in the near future. We do know the behaviors that create risk of exposure to the virus. Thus, people can avoid behavior that would put others at risk if they know they are HIV-positive. Hence, there is a need for additional testing in order to reduce risky behavior and therefore reduce the spread of HIV.

In addition to protecting others against infection, testing can help those who are infected begin intervention earlier. The use of drugs such as azidothymidine (AZT) and other treatments can lengthen and/or improve the quality of remaining life. Early knowledge may help those infected accept their situation more easily, and enable them to live their remaining years to the fullest. Recently, studies have indicated another benefit of knowledge of HIV status: it has been found that AZT substantially reduces the rate of transmission of HIV from an infected mother to her child in utero. Thus, for public health and personal reasons, greater testing is desirable.

Finally, home HIV tests would allow people not only to ascertain their own HIV status, but also allow them to significantly reduce their risk of exposure from a potentially infected partner. For instance, if two people enter into a long-term monogamous sexual relationship, each person could reduce their risk of exposure to HIV through their potential partner by up to 99.9% by having their partner use the home HIV test. (A time lapse does exist where HIV infection is not picked up by HIV antibody testing. This window usually lasts four to six weeks and at least 95% of infections will show up within six months.) This reduction of risk is notably better than that afforded by condoms, which reduce the risk of exposure between seventy and ninety percent. (It must be noted that condoms provide protection on a continual basis, while the home test would provide protection as long as the partners remained monogamous.)

Although existing clinics funded by state and federal government provide free AIDS testing, they are unable to handle the demand for such testing. In 1994, it is estimated that over five million requests for testing were placed at these clinics. There are often waits as long as two to six weeks to receive testing, and an additional one to four weeks for the results. Not only is the supply of testing not keeping up with the demand, but in many areas, especially those that are less densely populated, there are few or no clinics at all. The home HIV test would help the supply of available testing meet the existing demand.

COUNSELING ISSUES

The most criticized aspect of the home HIV test is the quality of the counseling the user receives on hearing the results of the test. The American Psychological Association, although it supports the concept of home HIV testing, is concerned about the counseling aspect, and would like a careful study of the issue. As there is no cure available, a person receiving a positive test result must face what some might consider to be a death sentence. Many argue that people receiving such devastating news need face-to-face counseling. In fact, there has been at least one reported case of a person who committed suicide after receiving news that he was HIV-positive. Those who hear of their status over the phone may hang up before receiving necessary counseling. A person, knowing that a counselor will give news of a positive test, may hang up if the phone wait is long, inferring that the wait stems from the unavailability of a counselor and therefore that he or she is HIV-positive. Opponents of home testing argue that the use of face-to-face counseling can prevent such results, and better inform people what it means to be HIV-positive.

Phone counseling resulting in suicide or suicide attempts represents a small yet serious risk. Inadequate counseling may result in the less dramatic but still serious harm of people not fully understanding the implications of an HIV-positive test result. Inadequate counseling may result from a home HIV test taker hanging up before or during counseling, or the counselor's inability to note the reactions of the test user and whether the user is absorbing the information provided by the counselor.

As a result of inadequate counseling, the user may not know that false positives occur. Subsequent testing may reveal that the test result was a false positive. Such a person might not learn that the dormancy period for HIV averages around ten years, or that drugs such as AZT can lengthen life expectancy, or at least improve quality of life. The availability of medical, psychological, and legal services may remain unknown to those with HIV who have not received adequate counseling.

Although opponents of the home test are critical of the counseling it provides, the demand on clinics providing HIV testing has lowered the quality of counseling at these clinics. A 1994 Centers for Disease Control (CDC) survey indicated that thirty-one percent of people who had been tested received their results by phone or mail, and eighty-five percent of those tested received no post-test counseling at all. Those using the home test will receive their results over the phone, like many already do, and will receive counseling from trained HIV counselors, which most people currently do not receive.

A Useful Tool

The spirited debate over whether a home access test for HIV should be licensed has not centered primarily on the test itself, which is quite accurate and reliable when laboratory quality-assurance guidelines are followed. The sticking point has been the adequacy of the telephone counseling associated with home access testing. The most quotable objection came from an HIV counselor who noted that "an 800 line can't hug you when you're crying."

Yet, for a certain segment of the population, the very remoteness and anonymity of telephone counseling is what makes the home-testing option attractive. Many years of experience with suicide and crisis-intervention hotlines point to telephone counseling as a potentially useful tool.

Jeff Stryker, *Priorities*, vol. 7, no. 3, 1995.

Additionally, phone counseling has proved to be effective in other areas. Suicide hot lines are an example of the effective use of phone counseling. Over ten million people a year receive counseling on such hot lines. Furthermore, AIDS hot lines have successfully provided counseling and information on services to HIV-positive individuals. To ensure the best possible phone counseling, the counselors for the Direct Access Diagnostics home HIV test will be guided by a computer program developed by Thom Moseley, who managed the AIDS hot line in Los Angeles. After studying the program, Martin Delaney, the director of the AIDS information group, Project Inform, declared it "bulletproof as any system." According to psychologist Thomas Coates, director of the Center for AIDS Prevention Studies at the University of California at San Francisco, the available evidence does not support concerns that telephone notification causes severe psychological reactions in people when they are told of their HIV-positive status.

Furthermore, some people may actually prefer dealing with a counselor anonymously and over the phone, as opposed to face-to-face. The fact that approximately twenty-five percent of those tested at clinics do not return for their results is evidence of many people's dislike of face-to-face counseling. Additionally, thirty percent of those who did not return for their results said they would use a home HIV test. Thus, it appears that phone counseling can provide a satisfactory alternative to face-to-face counseling that may be more attractive to many people than current counseling, and of better quality in many cases.

CONCERNS ABOUT ABUSE

Opponents of the home HIV test are concerned about possible abuses of testing by businesses and insurers. For example, an HIV-positive result might be used to deny a person employment or insurance. However, concerns about abuse by insurers are inflated. Insurers rarely engage in testing or underwriting for medical insurance. Additionally, because there is little legislation against such testing by insurers, the incentive to test without consent is not that great. If the insurer wants to determine a person's HIV status, it can request permission to test. If the person refuses, the insurer simply refuses to insure that person. If HIV testing by insurers were illegal, then a strong incentive to test without consent would exist.

Opponents of the home test claim it would create a greater incentive for HIV testing without consent by decreasing the cost of testing, and removing the health care professional from the process. The financial incentive to discover a person's HIV status exists because the cost of medical treatment for a person with HIV can be expensive. Those with access to a blood sample yielding the necessary three drops of blood could utilize the home test. Businesses often have access to such blood samples during pre-employment or annual physicals. It is true that if a business has withdrawn blood for testing purposes it could also test without consent using the traditional method. However, it would require a larger blood sample, cost more, and probably require at least the tacit consent of the health care professional who has drawn the blood. Whether these differences are enough to entice more businesses to test illegally remains to be seen. Nonetheless, home HIV tests provide the potential for businesses to illegally discriminate against people with HIV.

It would be difficult to discover an employer's improper testing without the business taking action based on the result. Under a normal testing procedure, there may be evidence of test samples being sent to a lab or test results being sent back to the business, such as a lab bill. With a home test, there is no method of determining who sent the sample in and who called for the results. Additionally, to provide such a method would reduce the desirability of the test, because anonymity would be lost. Nonconsensual testing through the use of a home test by a business must be shown through circumstantial evidence, which although more difficult, is possible.

Despite these difficulties, the potential for such abuse is not great. The use of a home test without a person's consent would violate the informed consent statutes of many states. Additionally, a federal district court has held that where an action based on an informed consent statute was not available, causes of action for battery, negligence, and negligent infliction of emotional harm were possible against an insurer who tested without consent.

Additionally, the Americans with Disabilities Act of 1990 (ADA) provides relief against the discriminatory use of HIV information. Under the ADA, no employer shall "discriminate against a qualified individual with a disability because of the disability of such individual in regard to job application procedures, the hiring, advancement, or discharge of employees." The legislative history of the ADA indicates that Congress considered HIV to be a disability under the Act. Thus, an employer cannot discriminate against HIV-positive employees. . . .

OTHER CONCERNS

Those who are critical of home tests argue that the tests, estimated to cost thirty to fifty dollars, will be too expensive for people with low incomes, including many minorities. Moreover, minorities also have the United States's fastest growing HIV infection rate. Thus, many of those at greatest risk will be unable to afford the test. Critics fear that test manufacturers will target the "worried well" able to afford thirty to fifty dollars, playing on their AIDS fears, even though many people in this group, by definition, are not of high risk. Hence, the benefits of the test will not be directed at those with the strongest need for such testing.

Despite these criticisms, home HIV tests may actually help expand testing among minority populations. There is support for home testing in many minority communities. Minorities tend to be more distrustful of authority, including the medical establishment, and thus less likely to be tested at a clinic or a doctor's office. A home HIV test would be attractive because of greater anonymity, and because there is no doctor or other health care professional with whom to interact. Since minorities have the fastest growing infection rate in the U.S., any increase in the amount of testing done in these communities would be beneficial. . . .

The home HIV test is not risk-free. In a perfect world, quality face-to-face counseling would be available for all who are tested. However, most people do not currently receive face-to-face counseling and many people do not want face-to-face counseling. In a perfect world, home tests would be immune to abuse. In the real world, abuse may occur, but there is legislation that guards against it. Ideally, the home test would be affordable to all, but free HIV testing is already available and the home test provides an option to many of those unsatisfied with current options.

By requiring basic demographic questions to be answered, the home HIV test can provide necessary information for effective epidemiology and public education campaigns. Although the perfect home test would be foolproof, the home test considered is very simple and provides practically no room for error. Finally, although some people may be embarrassed to buy the home HIV test, there is evidence that people will use the test, and those that use the test will benefit from it.

When the risks and benefits are balanced, the conclusion reached is that the FDA should approve the home HIV test. The strongest factor to consider is that information is the only weapon against AIDS. The home test provides people with the information they need so as to avoid behavior that risks spreading HIV. If the home HIV test can increase the number of people tested and provide quality counseling, and the evidence indicates it can, its approval is a step in the fight against AIDS that must be taken.

| "The potential for catastrophic impact on individuals using, or being coerced to use, an HIV home test product far outweighs the intended advantages."

HOME HIV TESTS ARE UNETHICAL

Christopher J. Portelli

In July 1996, the Food and Drug Administration approved the sale and use of home test kits to determine HIV status. In the following viewpoint, which was written prior to the approval of the kits, Christopher J. Portelli contends that the risks associated with home HIV tests outweigh the benefits. He argues that delivering test results by telephone is unethical and that phone counseling does not provide adequate support for people who test positive for HIV. Furthermore, he maintains that some people may be coerced or forced to take the test, which would violate their right to privacy. Portelli is the executive director of the National Lesbian and Gay Health Association in Washington, D.C.

As you read, consider the following questions:

1. In the author's opinion, why is it inappropriate to compare home HIV tests to home pregnancy or home cholesterol tests?
2. How does home HIV testing defeat the purpose of the Ryan White Care Act, according to Portelli?
3. Who might coerce individuals to use the home HIV tests against their will, in Portelli's opinion?

From Christopher J. Portelli, "Should the FDA Approve HIV Home Test Kits? No," *Priorities*, no. 3, 1995. Reprinted with permission from *Priorities*, a publication of the American Council on Science and Health, 1995 Broadway, 2nd Floor, New York, NY 10023-5860.

Despite the possibility that HIV home testing may increase the number of individuals being tested for HIV, and despite the possibility that increased numbers of HIV-positive individuals who are identified may seek earlier treatment and modify their sexual practices, the potential for catastrophic impact on individuals using, or being coerced to use, an HIV home test product far outweighs the intended advantages. Comparisons to home pregnancy test kits or home cholesterol tests do not stand up: Neither pregnancy tests nor cholesterol tests detect a life-threatening, sexually transmitted disease for which there is as yet no known cure.

THE PRODUCTS

If the FDA [Food and Drug Administration] approves HIV home test kits, a consumer will purchase a test kit over the counter at a local drugstore. [The FDA approved home HIV tests in July 1996.] The kit contains brochures about HIV and AIDS, detailed instructions about how to use the kit, a blood-sample collection device (usually a disposable lancet) and a swab of treated paper. The lances enables the user to draw a few drops of blood from a finger; the swab absorbs the blood sample. A mailer is provided along with an individual ID number. In four to 10 days after dropping the blood sample into the mail, the test user will call for results, punching in his or her personal ID number. The test user/caller will then obtain negative results either from a live operator or from a recording; positive results will come from a live operator.

If the test result is positive, the operator will give the caller "counseling information" about the positive result and provide a list of resources and HIV/AIDS service organizations in the user's geographic area. Some manufacturers have stated that their operators will be "trained counselors," but no standards for such counselors have been discussed or put forward.

EXTREME ADVERSE REACTIONS

There is a very real increased risk of serious psychological trauma, including severe depression and increased incidence of suicide, for HIV-positive individuals who discover their serostatus at home without the benefit of one-on-one and face-to-face counseling by trained professionals. There is a well-established clinical record of extreme adverse reaction to the news of HIV-positive status.

Marshall Forstein, M.D., Director of HIV Mental Health Services for the Department of Psychiatry at The Cambridge Hospital and Chair of the American Psychiatric Association's Commission on AIDS, has stated that inadequate psychological resources are a significant contributory factor for increased HIV-related suicide during key phases of HIV testing: in the pretest phase, during the testing process and at the time of determination of HIV status (receipt of a positive diagnosis) as well as during the course of HIV infection.

A FALSE SENSE OF SECURITY

Studies have shown that testing negative for H.I.V. can create a false sense of confidence in many people. A test that allows people to evade health care professionals could allow that false confidence to soar. It could become a sort of "morning after" routine that seduces us into believing we're safe—until, eventually, we call the 800 number and get a real voice on the phone.

Michelangelo Signorile, New York Times, May 25, 1996.

HIV counselors report that many persons have an initial adverse reaction to the news that they are HIV positive. People with HIV report that they experienced a phase during which they seriously considered quitting their jobs and leaving their homes to drink, drug and despair. Fortunately, through counseling, compassion, support and follow-up care from health-care professionals and volunteers, many of these same people with HIV forego such drastic action and begin dealing with their infection.

An individual who tests at home and confronts a positive test result alone, and who has little or no access to counseling or medical care, will also have little or no real information to assuage even normal fears about the future. Is this informed consent? Does this truly facilitate getting people the medical and mental health care they need to deal with the news of their HIV status? Based on the established Centers for Disease Control and Prevention (CDC) and Agency for Health Care Policy Research (AHCPR) standards for HIV testing, counseling and the delivery of test results, the answer to these questions is a resounding "no."

STANDARDS AND GUIDELINES

As federal agencies charged with the public health and safety of all American citizens, the CDC and AHCPR are well situated to gather experts, conduct research, present data and establish criteria for the safe and effective management of HIV disease. The Food and Drug Administration, when evaluating home HIV testing products, should follow CDC and AHCPR standards of care.

The FDA should uphold those standards when determining whether a home test product is safe and effective; and the FDA cannot and should not ignore the standards the CDC and AHCPR have established for HIV testing, counseling, and delivery of test results as set forth in the guidelines published by those agencies since January of 1993.

The AHCPR Guidelines state that HIV pretest and posttest counseling and the disclosure of test results should all take place face-to-face. The CDC requires that "HIV counseling must be client-centered" and must be conducted by counselors in a manner that is "culturally competent . . .; sensitive to issues of sexual identity . . .; developmentally appropriate . . .; [and] linguistically specific. . . ."

The AHCPR Guidelines specify that when hearing HIV-positive results, persons availing themselves of testing services should have the opportunity to discuss the natural history of HIV infection, the potential effects of HIV infection on physical and mental health, the prevention of further HIV transmission and the role of health maintenance. Most significantly, the AHCPR recommends that HIV test results for adolescents be given in the presence of a supportive adult or close friend.

There is an inherent risk of adolescents' end children's gaining access to over-the-counter test kits and seeking their serostatus without the knowledge or support necessary to handle an HIV-positive result (or without full understanding of a negative result). Teenagers and children could be emotionally and psychologically damaged by the results without immediate help on hand. It is not excessive to say that young lives could be destroyed, literally as well as figuratively.

TELEPHONE DIAGNOSES

The outcome of an HIV test is commonly referred to as a "test result." It is also the diagnosis of a potentially life-threatening medical condition. Medical practitioners will tell you that to deliver such a significant diagnosis by telephone is inappropriate and possibly unethical. Were we to have a diagnostic test for heart disease or breast cancer, who would seriously advocate that the diagnosis be provided over the telephone? That being the case, why are we considering institutionalizing this practice with the virus that causes AIDS?

Not even negative test results should be delivered over the telephone—much less by recorded message. A negative result can create a false sense of security, and that will not be counteracted by printed matter provided as a substitute for precounseling.

Seronegative persons who do not receive, heed or understand the pretest counseling information—particularly information regarding the "window" issue (the six-week to six-month period following exposure to HIV during which antibodies may not be detected in the blood)—will be placed at greater risk. And faulty safer sex practices will subject numerous others to an increased risk of HIV infection.

Among those people who test HIV positive, the risks created by misinformation, panic and denial are greatly increased for those who do not have the benefit of direct, face-to-face counseling. According to Marion Brown, Director of HIV Counseling and Testing at Whitman Walker Clinic in Washington, DC, these are legitimate concerns based on years of clinical experience. Brown says, "I shiver when I think of people getting tested for HIV without the benefit of face-to-face pretest counseling and then receiving their test results over the phone. Hearing an HIV test result over the phone isn't a healthy experience even for those who test negative. HIV testing involves more than learning one's HIV status. The counseling provided assists those who are negative in changing their behavior to remain negative."

THE LAW

The manufacturers of HIV home tests disregard the development of the law and the intent of Congress and state legislatures on HIV/AIDS, especially regarding such matters as early intervention, informed consent, privacy, confidentiality and discrimination.

In creating the Ryan White Care Act [a program that provides funds to cities to help them cope with the impact of AIDS], for example, Congress strove to create a continuum of care so that individuals who sought counseling and testing would have immediate access at the same site to early intervention and prevention case management. HIV home testing defeats this important legislative purpose. The CDC protocols regarding HIV testing and counseling services also mandate that face-to-face counseling and primary-care services be available at the test site. These precautions are the direct result of battles fought and won by AIDS activists almost 10 years ago. Why are we quick to rewrite these laws and abandon these policies now?

Many states mandate anonymous testing, confidentiality and standards for informed consent. But home test kit manufacturers have been lobbying state legislatures to change laws the activist community worked so hard to put in place. Why undo these laws to allow for this kind of testing and disclosure? Will manufacturers be required to report those who test seropositive to contact-tracing agencies in those states that mandate such reporting?

VIOLENCE AND COERCION

The increased risk of violence directed toward partners and family members who test positive while at home is very real. The National Association of People with AIDS found in their 1992 study *HIV In America* that 21 percent of HIV-positive individuals surveyed nationwide already had experienced violence in their communities because of their HIV status; 27 percent of HIV-positive African Americans had experienced such violence. The study also found that 25 percent of HIV-positive Latina women had experienced violence in the home because of their HIV status and that 24 percent of HIV-positive bisexual men had experienced violence in the home because of their status.

What will these statistics look like if parents or partners suspicious of their child's or their spouse's sexual activity outside the home start bringing home HIV test kits and demanding that family members test? The potential for violence, particularly violence against women, due to household members forcing individuals to take the test, surrender the code number and call for results is a serious concern.

The home test kit also bears a substantial risk for abuse and misuse outside the home. Employers, insurance companies, law-enforcement officials, school administrators and untrained counselors—just to name a few—might coerce individuals to test against their will or might commandeer code numbers to obtain test results without voluntary consent. What controls will be devised to prevent coerced testing on the job? Legislation may exist to provide HIV-positive people a redress for their claims of discrimination based on HIV status, but how many of those people will have the opportunity to challenge an employer, a parent or a law-enforcement official who coerces them to test and then denies them their rights on the basis of the results?

ACCESS TO SERVICES IN RURAL AREAS

The argument is often made that the populations who would benefit most from home HIV testing products are those in remote or isolated areas of the country, including those in rural communities. But access to a test device alone does not increase access to testing and treatment services without the concerted effort and involvement of community leaders and local consumers. If test manufacturers are genuinely concerned about the course of HIV disease in rural communities, there are various actions they can take to increase services in these areas through the careful marketing of their product.

Only true innovation and community partnerships with industry will bring the care and treatment needed to stem the tide of HIV in rural areas. Test kit manufacturers could contract with local therapists, physicians or other health-care professionals who could be trained to do posttest counseling and give results in their communities. Manufacturers could provide grants for local community health centers to do posttest counseling and give results in a local clinic or doctor's office.

FOLLOW-UP CARE IS NECESSARY

There are no "quick fixes" to the problems of accessibility to effective counseling and testing and to adequate follow-up care. The problem of access, both to competent test sites and to adequate follow-up care, will not be solved simply by increasing testing alone. There is a need for increased testing, counseling and early intervention services, especially for minorities and women. The danger is in losing sight of the real issues and allowing the availability of technology and greed to cloud judgment.

To date, not a single manufacturer has addressed any of these concerns. Instead, the manufacturers point to their marketing statistics, which reveal only how popular their products will be, predominantly among the "worried well" who will be their prime target. Theirs is not the provision of a public service, however, no matter how slick the marketing campaigns or how many tests the manufacturers intend to distribute for "free." As long as the home test manufacturers refuse to sit down with the testers themselves and begin to work on the very real problems their products will create, theirs is only a get-rich-quick scheme—a scheme that targets the most vulnerable populations caught up in the HIV pandemic: the poor, the isolated and the oppressed.

"Mandatory testing is necessary
because every patient has the
absolute right to know what harm
can befall him or her from a health
care worker."

HEALTH CARE WORKERS SHOULD BE TESTED FOR HIV

Sanford F. Kuvin

In 1990, the Centers for Disease Control and Prevention announced that a dentist with AIDS in Florida appeared to have infected five of his patients, one of whom was a twenty-two-year-old woman named Kimberly Bergalis. The announcement provoked a fierce debate over whether health care workers should be tested for HIV. The following viewpoint is excerpted from Sanford F. Kuvin's testimony before the House Subcommittee on Health and Environment, in which he argues that all health care workers should be tested for the AIDS virus. Patients have the right to know if their doctor, nurse, dentist, or other health care professional has HIV, he maintains. Kuvin is the vice chairman of the National Foundation for Infectious Diseases and chairman of the Hepatitis B Action Group in Washington, D.C.

As you read, consider the following questions:

1. Why are the Centers for Disease Control and Prevention's universal precautions for HIV infection control ineffective, according to Kuvin?
2. What evidence does the author present to support his contention that voluntary testing and disclosure have failed?
3. In Kuvin's opinion, how is HIV/AIDS being treated as a secret disease?

Excerpted from Sanford F. Kuvin, statement before the House Subcommittee on Health and the Environment, Committee on Energy and Commerce, 102nd Cong., 1st sess., September 26, 1991.

For the very first time in medical history, health care providers who are carriers of the human immunodeficiency virus (HIV) or hepatitis B are being viewed as a risk group capable of transmitting lethal diseases to their patients.

The guidelines of the Centers for Disease Control (CDC) call for the voluntary testing of health care workers carrying out exposure-prone procedures, do not recommend mandatory patient testing to protect the health care worker, and rely only on improved infection control and universal precautions. These guidelines fail to protect the patient and the health care worker alike by not calling for mandatory testing for HIV and hepatitis B for health care workers and patients undergoing invasive procedures.

PRECAUTIONS ARE NOT ENOUGH

The universal precautions called for by the CDC, including improved infection control, did not, do not, and will not provide for universal safety. Gloves leak, puncture and rip, and the cognitive and motor skills of infected health care workers will always be subject to mistakes. In addition, approximately 30 to 40 percent of all patients with HIV develop clinically discernable neurologic symptoms at any stage of the infection. Therefore, HIV-infected health care workers will develop AIDS Dementia Complex which is characterized by motor disturbances and behavioral disorders. AIDS Dementia Complex causes mistakes of judgement and manual dexterity by the invasive health care worker leading to the additional spread of HIV and hepatitis B and other blood-borne diseases to patients.

Physicians and dentists have an absolute moral, ethical, professional and legal obligation not to cause harm to a patient. Mandatory testing is necessary because every patient has the absolute right to know what harm can befall him or her from a health care worker, and conversely, every health care worker has that same right to know. Blood is a two-way street and health care workers are, in fact, at much greater risk than patients. Both need protection against each other not provided for in the CDC guidelines.

Voluntary testing called for by the CDC, the American Medical Association, and the American Dental Association has failed. Failed voluntarism is exactly what caused the five patients to be infected [by dentist David Acer] in Florida. Failed voluntarism has caused the almost weekly revelations about AIDS-infected dentists and physicians across this nation failing to voluntarily tell their patients they had AIDS or HIV.

There are over 6,000 health care workers with AIDS, about 50,000 with HIV, and thousands more with hepatitis B—and the epidemic is expanding. Will the thousands of health care workers who are carriers of HIV or hepatitis B voluntarily reveal their serological status to their patients or their peers? Will any member of this Subcommittee voluntarily send their spouse, their child, or their grandchild to an HIV- or hepatitis B-infected invasive health care worker? I think not!

PART OF A COMPREHENSIVE PROGRAM

U.S. public health policy during the first decade of the AIDS epidemic has been a disaster. A comprehensive, federally directed AIDS program should have been in place years ago, a program based on absolute non-discrimination. The infected person's economic and social well-being must be guaranteed. With this as a preamble, a national program would then address the epidemic through epidemiologic methods, employing all the traditional weapons used in the past, including mandatory testing where necessary, full reportability, and contact tracing. Questions as to whether or not an HIV-positive HCW [health care worker] should practice would be addressed in short order by such an approach: No.

Ralph E. Dittman, *Priorities*, Fall 1991.

Mandatory testing is already in place for all of our blood donors, all of our military, all our prisoners, our job corps, all immigrants, and all foreign service employees as well as our life insurance policies. Surely the American people deserve that same kind of protection since the health care setting is where the majority of Americans face their only risk of contracting HIV or hepatitis B. This small but significant number of patients infected from their health care worker—just like Kimberly Bergalis [one of Acer's patients]—are totally unaware of their being infected with a lethal disease which is preventable. Liability insurers and hospital employers will demand mandatory testing in any event for malpractice coverage.

A SECRET DISEASE

Seventy-six percent of HIV cases occur in 22 states where HIV is nonreportable. This is the first time in the history of our public health system that a lethal communicable disease is being treated as a secret disease. If you can't test for HIV you can't trace it. And If you can't trace it you can't treat it. And if you can't treat HIV/AIDS you cannot prolong life. Confidentiality laws can and will be maintained. Our Public Health Service and our private medical sector have a 100-year proud tradition of maintaining confidentiality, and if necessary, additional laws can be made so punitive that confidentiality will be maintained.

ELIMINATE THE THREAT

Kimberly Bergalis is certainly not the first case of HIV transmission from health care worker to patient. Kimberly is the first *documented* case utilizing DNA high technology which was never available before in medical history. This is the reason why this one cluster of cases is driving a change in public health policy. This is the reason why you do not wait for a second 747 to crash when you know the cause of the first one. And this is the reason why you test airline pilots and subway motormen once a year and on demand for alcohol and drugs. This same schedule of once-a-year and on-demand testing linked to professional licensure would remove over 95% of infected health care workers with HIV and hepatitis B as a reservoir of infection—which is basic public health. You do not treat a typhoid epidemic in a restaurant by cleaning the utensils. You remove "Typhoid Mary" from the kitchen. And you do not treat a malaria epidemic by putting mosquito netting around the beds—you eliminate the malaria-carrying mosquito. Public health and organized medical leadership has been medically anachronistic in medical logic concerning basic public health approaches to the expanding HIV epidemic. And if anyone says that the risk of HIV transmission is "remote" or "essentially nil" as articulated by former surgeon general Dr. C. Everett Koop, then ask Kimberly Bergalis or Barbara Webb [another of Acer's patients] or Dr. Edward Rozar [a physician infected by his HIV-positive patient] or any of the 40 health care workers infected with AIDS, and hundreds more infected with HIV from patients. They will all tell you that their risk was 100%. And what about the paradigm of hepatitis B which is of equal importance and an example of a blood-borne virus 100 times more infectious with 7,000 health care workers in 1990 getting hepatitis B from their patients and with almost 250 dying? The risk of HIV transmission is indeed small, but the results are definite, devastating, lethal and entirely avoidable in the health care setting by simply removing the reservoir of infection—the infected invasive health care worker.

MANDATORY TESTING

Testing is getting better, quicker, and cheaper all the time. . . . The biotechnology of testing is far ahead of public health, and industry has ample profit motive to bring the cost of testing down. The Food and Drug Administration (FDA) should pursue the issue of licensing rapid diagnostics for HIV, which already exist, with as much expediency as possible. Modern medicine demands that testing be done as a routine procedure to discover, prevent and treat disease in all parameters of medicine. For example, in our own blood supply mandatory testing is carried out for syphilis, HIV, HTLV I/II (human T cell lymphotropic virus—a leukemia producing virus), hepatitis B and hepatitis C. Mammograms, Pap smears, blood tests for diabetes, thyroid disorders, prostatic cancer, and a host of other tests are done regularly to discover, treat and prevent disease. Are all people diagnosed with disease treated? Certainly not, but surely that is the very goal of medical discovery. It is not only bad medicine, but it is bad public health to continue to single out and treat HIV as a secret disease in the health care worker and the patient which prohibits the fundamental medical right to test for HIV for the purposes of discovery which is necessary to prevent and treat this disease.

LEGISLATION IS NECESSARY

Legislation at the congressional and state levels and rule making at the regulatory level of the Occupational Safety and Health Administration (OSHA) are necessary to protect health care providers and patients against the risk of blood-borne pathogens. In addition, government and insurers have a responsibility to respond to the economic hardships that occupationally infected health care workers face when, by virtue of adhering to the CDC guidelines of no patient testing for HIV or hepatitis B, they are forced out of business after being infected from patients. Invasive health care workers including medical, dental, and nursing students, residents, house staff and other health care workers should be covered with some form of economic indemnification for disability, workers compensation, life and health insurance, alternative job placement and retraining programs as well as other mechanisms that compensate for the risk they face from infected patients with HIV and hepatitis B. . . .

The central principle of medicine is still "First do no harm." How can a physician or dentist know that he or she will do no harm when he or she is a carrier of HIV, hepatitis B or any other blood-borne disease?

| "A policy of mandatory HIV testing for health care workers violates their rights to privacy and self-determination and cannot be justified."

MANDATORY TESTING OF HEALTH CARE WORKERS IS UNJUSTIFIED

Keith Berndtson

In the following viewpoint, Keith Berndtson argues that mandatory testing of health care workers and patients is unethical, wasteful, and unnecessary. There is very little risk of HIV transmission in health care settings, he maintains, and that risk could be lowered further by scrupulous adherence to safety precautions. In addition, he contends, mandatory testing of health care workers or patients violates constitutional rights and could lead to discrimination against those who test HIV positive. Berndtson is the medical director of Rush Corporate Health Center in Chicago.

As you read, consider the following questions:
1. What is the ratio of Americans infected with HIV, according to Berndtson?
2. What is the prevalence of HIV in health care workers compared to the general population, according to the Centers for Disease Control and Prevention, as cited by the author?
3. In Berndtson's opinion, why is it pointless to screen emergency room patients for HIV?

Excerpted from Keith Berndtson, "Mandatory HIV Testing and the Character of Medicine," *Second Opinion*, January 1994. Reprinted by permission of the Park Ridge Center, Chicago, Illinois. (Notes in the original have been omitted here.)

Feelings are part of everyday human reality, and when it comes to settling conflicts about values, reality has a way of getting the last word. If we want ethics to confront reality, then we want ethics to confront how emotions shape our value judgments and motivate our behaviors. Consider the following two examples.

Imagine that I show you a family portrait: a mother, a father, a preschool daughter, and an infant son. I tell you that the father got infected with the human immunodeficiency virus (HIV), which moved through his wife to his son. Then I tell you that all three died of the acquired immunodeficiency syndrome (AIDS). Then I tell you that the father was a closet homosexual. You register a response.

If I tell you instead that the father was a surgeon who contracted HIV on the job, is your response different? Even the simplest human stories are value-laden, and these values prompt feelings that occur before we've had a chance to pause and reflect. Rational thinking begins after we react emotionally to the facts.

Example two. You're in the hospital with acute appendicitis, and the surgeon whom you would prefer tells you that she is HIV-positive, and that, based on current estimates, the highest risk of getting infected from the procedure is 1 in 28,000 per hour of surgery. Would you want a different surgeon? You'd certainly think about it. Even if you counted up to 28,000 by ones, you'd think about it. When doing ethics, we should acknowledge that emotions are part of the picture.

THE RELEVANT FACTS

Where should an ethical inquiry begin? Most analyses are informed by theory, and most theories of ethics can be boiled down to their first questions. Aristotle, for example, began with the questions "What is my purpose?" and "What is good?" Kant began with the questions "What is my duty?" and "What is right?" My favorite first question comes from an ethical tradition rounded by the theologian H. Richard Niebuhr, who began by asking "What is going on?"

This question focuses our attention on getting the facts relevant to the issue at hand. It also reminds us that, whatever the issue, we had best stand humble before the possibility that a higher power may hold us accountable for how we choose to act with what we are given. For purposes of this discussion, we are given a devil of a retrovirus that is exceptionally good at ruining human lives.

By the end of 1992, over 13 million people around the world had been infected with HIV. Roughly 3 million have developed

AIDS, and of these, over 90 percent have died. As many as one million Americans are thought to be infected with HIV. That's one in every 250 of us, most of whom are destined to suffer from AIDS within 10 years. Well over 100 million could be infected worldwide by the year 2000. We have seen more than enough HIV-related suffering to know that something must be done to control this pandemic. We also know that control measures have a greater payoff when they are taken earlier rather than later in the course of an epidemic. What role, if any, should mandatory HIV testing play in our fight against the spread of AIDS?

HIV TRANSMISSION RISKS

To decide whether the mandatory testing of patients or health care workers for HIV is ethical, we need to know something about the risks of transmitting the virus in health care settings. HIV is not spread through the air or water. It is not passed along the fecal-oral pathway or by insects. HIV is blood-borne, and there appears to be but one method for transmission by various routes: the commingling of certain body fluids, be it via sex, intravenous drug abuse, transfusion, or other forms of contact.

It is in the health care setting that we are most concerned about these other forms of contact: needlesticks, other injuries from sharps, or exposure of infected fluid to non-intact skin or mucous membranes. If such exposures happen in emergency rooms, operating rooms, and other health care settings every day, does routine, involuntary screening of patients or health care workers make sense from a public health perspective? If so, what are the ethical implications?

One study in a Baltimore hospital in 1987 found that 3 percent of all emergency room patients were HIV-positive and that they accounted for 16 percent of patients seen because of trauma. Yet the 1989 AIDS Case Surveillance System of the Centers for Disease Control and Prevention shows that the prevalence of HIV in health care workers is roughly the same as in the general population, suggesting little or no occupational hazard. More recent reports, however, suggest a small but as yet undetermined occupational risk to health care workers. This occupational risk appears to be more strongly related to the frequency of occupational exposures than to the infectiousness of the virus, which is generally thought to be quite low. Several postexposure studies suggest that the risk of transmitting HIV from infected patients to health care workers is about one per 300 exposures.

We can tentatively conclude that transmitting HIV from patients to health care workers in an occupational setting is almost entirely preventable through the disciplined use of universal precautions, increased alertness when using sharps, and attentiveness to detail when performing invasive procedures. But if surgery, emergency medicine, and other health care work involving invasive procedures are more prone to result in the commingling of body fluids, should we consider routine testing of patients in these environments? We can scratch emergency room patients from the list because, to be useful, screening requires lead time during which corrective action can presumably take place. But what about hospitalized patients, or at least patients scheduled for elective procedures?

A MINUTE RISK

The CDC [Centers for Disease Control and Prevention] has estimated that "1 out of every 263,100 to 2,631,000 dental procedures results in 1 case of HIV transmission, [and] 1 out of every 41,600 to 416,000 surgical procedures results in 1 case of HIV infection." In contrast, one out of every 10,000 persons undergoing general anesthesia dies, one to two out of every 100,000 persons who receive penicillin die as a result of an adverse reaction, and one out of 15,385 women die from pregnancy-related complications. When compared to other risks patients face when receiving health care, the risk of contracting HIV from a seropositive HCP [health care professional] is minute.

HCPs who cut or puncture themselves during surgery "do not necessarily expose the patient to their blood," according to Lawrence Gostin. For transmission to occur, the HIV-positive HCP "would have to sustain an injury and bleed into a patient's wound, or after sustaining an injury during an invasive procedure, have the sharp object causing the injury then recontact the patient's open wound or otherwise nonintact skin, resulting in the patient's exposure to the health care [professional's] blood," according to the National Commission on AIDS. However, because a small amount of contaminated blood is unlikely to transmit HIV, this form of transmission is unlikely to occur as long as the proper sterilization and universal precaution techniques are observed.

Susan L. DiMaggio, *American Journal of Law & Medicine*, vol. XIX, no. 4, 1993.

Physicians in Illinois can test patients for HIV without their consent if they believe that it is in the patient's best interest to do so. Granting legal sanction for selective, involuntary screening would appear less ethically problematic than widespread mandatory testing, but this policy is no less vulnerable to criticism.

First, it permits resources to be wasted in indiscriminate testing, because most Americans (249 of 250) are not infected with HIV. Second, with all due respect to standard procedures, it is difficult to guarantee confidentiality about HIV-positive results, and this creates potential for HIV-related prejudice and discrimination. Third, physicians can easily confuse the patient's best interest with the desire to reduce their own anxiety, and no strong informed-consent safeguards are currently in place to protect the patient's rights. Fourth, selective screening may lower the incentive to observe universal precautions by providing false reassurance about HIV-negative status. Fifth, knowing a patient's HIV status is not required to improve adherence to universal precautions.

If these criticisms apply to a policy of selective testing without consent, they apply even more to a policy of mandatory testing without consent. As the epidemic unfolds, we may find ways to justify the selective, involuntary testing of certain patients in certain situations, but carte-blanche testing of patients for HIV without their consent appears morally reckless at best.

In performing mandatory testing of patients for HIV, then, we are making significant moral sacrifices—but for what? Insuring peace of mind for health care workers is a worthy goal, especially for those engaged in exposure-prone jobs, but it is also something of an illusion because of the problem of false-negative results. We should not waste scarce resources or trash long-standing ethical traditions in order to chase the illusion of a risk-free health care environment.

MANDATORY TESTING OF HEALTH CARE WORKERS

What about transmission from health care worker to patient? In 1991, Illinois governor James Edgar appointed a task force of experts to consider the merits of mandatory testing of health care workers for HIV, based on reports of HIV transmission from a Florida dentist to as many as five of his patients. This Florida case, however, despite dozens of retrospective studies involving thousands of patients potentially exposed via procedures performed by HIV-infected health care workers, remains the only documented case of transmission from a health care worker to a patient. Based on fairly extensive experience, the risk of accidental transmission from health care worker to patient is virtually nonexistent. This is not to say that groups of surgeons should never volunteer for periodic preexposure testing or routine postexposure testing, because such studies can incrementally advance our understanding of the transmission dynamics and occupational risks of working with HIV-positive patients. But these kinds of studies do not hold promise for major preventive breakthroughs.

A policy of mandatory HIV testing for health care workers violates their rights to privacy and self-determination and cannot be justified by claims concerning public welfare or epidemic control. It wastes resources, it creates false impressions about patient exposure-proneness from surgical procedures, it discriminates against surgeons and other health care personnel, and it creates unnecessary administrative and liability headaches for physicians and hospitals. In short, it's unethical. So why all the fuss?

POLITICS, LAW, AND PUBLIC HEALTH

There's a fuss because public health policy in the U.S. is driven more by political than by medical expediencies. Politicians naturally respond to their loudest and most powerful constituents. But HIV is making its way into the population via the disenfranchised, who are neither loud nor powerful. Public health policy seems driven by twin fears: the fear of AIDS and the fear that decision makers may alienate their constituents, most of whom lack sophistication about AIDS or epidemic control.

Thus far in the epidemic, there is a lesson for policymakers: while political insiders look to the polls for ways to win votes, outside, in the real world, HIV is being spread by citizens who don't get polled or simply don't vote: teens, addicts, prostitutes, and poor ethnic minorities. Transmission rates among homosexuals are decreasing, in large part because of the gay community's ability to organize preventive education efforts. But public health experts seem to spend more time slugging it out with a misinformed public than with the virus itself, and enlightening discussion tends to get drowned out by acrimonious debate. As is so often the case, medicine and ethics seem helpless spectators as one issue after another gets punted to the courts.

Courts will see the issue of mandatory testing as one of balancing private rights with the public interest. Two examples of court opinion serve as relevant precedents. In a famous case where a psychiatrist failed to warn a patient's girlfriend about his homicidal threats against her, the court ruled that "the protective privilege ends where the public peril begins" (*Tarasoff v. Regents of the University of California* 1976). But where, in the case of AIDS, does the public peril begin? At a risk of one in 28,000? One in 300? One in 250? In another landmark case which sought to determine where to draw the line concerning one's responsibility to foresee and prevent low-risk accidents, the court ruled that "the risk reasonably to be perceived defines the duty to be obeyed" (*Palsgraf v. Long Island Railroad* 1928). A risk of contracting HIV from an infected surgeon of one in 28,000 per hour of surgery is like having a gun with one bullet and 28,000 chambers pointed at your temple. How many people would have peace of mind about such a low risk if a gun was actually at their temple? Yet virtually every activity in life carries some risk of death. Ordinarily we don't think about our daily activities in these terms. The gun with many chambers is always there, whether we like it or not, but it's only when we're conscious of the danger that it threatens our peace of mind.

One problem with relying on the law to manage this epidemic is that we can't afford to wait for courts to point the way. Another problem is that the law seems to have an even harder time than ethics of making emotions part of the picture. But the fear of AIDS *belongs* in the picture. Behind our fear of AIDS is a fear as old as time about the triumph of death, and as the prevalence of HIV increases, so will our fears.

FEAR AND COURAGE

A policy of mandatory testing for HIV is a misguided attempt to escape the fears that we have about suffering and death. Mandatory testing would waste much, accomplish little, and trample ethical traditions along the way. If we want to be ethical, we're stuck dealing with an unpleasant emotion. What can we do with the fears we have about this virus?

Consider the parable of the lions. A shrewd pride of lions figured out a way to capture prey without having to work very hard. They sent the old toothless grandfather off to the far side of the plain, and the rest gathered behind the tall grass. Whenever potential prey came through the plain, the weak old lion would let loose a fearsome roar, and the prey would run straight into the clutches of death. The lesson, of course, is that we are better off facing our fears than running away from them. If we run away from our fears of HIV and AIDS, we will surely get ourselves into deeper trouble.

Once again, the problem isn't necessarily where the noise is. We need to wage war against drug abuse, unsafe sex, and the conditions that breed these behaviors. Our society can hardly be expected to wage an effective war against the AIDS virus if health care workers are being driven to distraction on the front lines by their own fears of HIV. . . .

An ethical analysis of mandatory HIV testing leads to a simple question about the character of medicine, namely, how do we inspire the courage needed to deal with the fear of AIDS?

In addressing this question, it is appropriate to consult the legacy of physician Benjamin Rush. It was Rush who said, "To spend and be spent for the good of mankind is what I chiefly aim at." Rush made his mark in history by inspiring others to virtue in both medicine and politics. Two hundred years ago Rush led the battle against a yellow fever epidemic in Philadelphia. His letters are the sole historical account of this devastating plague. It is obvious from his account that the risks to physicians at that time were great, but few, including Rush, backed away from their tasks. Rush may not have had the right idea about the causes or treatment of yellow fever (in fact, his ideas were way off), but he understood that physicians and caregivers over the ages have had to contend with the occupational risks of contracting disease, and that facing these risks required great courage. He also believed that, when it came to controlling fearsome infectious diseases, good public health policy should trump politics as usual. This too can take courage.

The threat of AIDS seems to have us spellbound. Meanwhile, the virus makes its way into more bodies and more lives. It's early in the epidemic, but the clock is ticking away on policies that stand to have their greatest impact if implemented now. If we don't step up our response, I dread to think what we'll be saying and feeling about this virus and our response to it 10 years from now.

We can start to break the spell by acknowledging and, where possible, emulating the physicians, nurses, and allied caregivers who observe universal precautions to the letter; by respecting and learning from those who make a special point of handling sharps with care at all times; by honoring those who, when they perform invasive procedures, are able to demonstrate the extreme attentiveness to detail that this virus demands; and by supporting those who take political risks for the sake of medically and morally sensible AIDS policies. These colleagues are modeling our most highly ethical response to HIV-related risks in the health care setting and in the broader social setting. When the medical community models this kind of courage and commitment, we can ask the rest of our society to do the same.

When we face our fears about AIDS courageously, we will be better able to balance private rights with the public interest. If we can inspire courage in each other as we work together to manage this epidemic, voluntary screening based on informed consent will be able to assume its rightful place as the ethical standard for HIV testing in all settings.

"[The] general nullification of health care professionals' duty to warn known . . . third-parties of . . . life-threatening danger seems unwarranted."

PARTNER NOTIFICATION OF HIV STATUS WOULD REDUCE THE SPREAD OF AIDS

Geoffrey A.D. Smereck

Partner notification, or contact tracing, is the identification and notification by health care workers of individuals who may have been exposed to an infectious disease. In the following viewpoint, Geoffrey A.D. Smereck asserts that although the AIDS epidemic presents many difficulties for contact tracing, this practice should still be utilized. Partner notification would cause those at risk of HIV infection to make significant changes in their behavior that could reduce the likelihood of their contracting or spreading HIV, Smereck argues. Laws or regulations that restrict health care workers' ability to warn third parties of their potential exposure to HIV are unjustified and unwarranted, he maintains. Smereck is the president of the Well-Being Institute in Ann Arbor, Michigan.

As you read, consider the following questions:

1. Public health officials have used contact tracing to combat the spread of which infectious diseases, according to the author?
2. According to Smereck, what are some of the problems inherent in contact tracing in the AIDS epidemic?

From Geoffrey A.D. Smereck, "Contact Tracing for HIV Infection: Policy and Program Implications from a Fifty-State Survey," *Drugs and Society*, no. 3/4, 1993. Copyright ©1993 by The Haworth Press. Reprinted by permission of the publisher, The Haworth Press, Binghamton, NY. (Notes in the original have been omitted here.)

The Acquired Immunodeficiency Syndrome (AIDS) epidemic, the most dangerous public health crisis in American history, continues its horrific assault. The causative Human Immunodeficiency Virus (HIV), which is transmitted via physical contact with infected blood and body fluids, continues to be spread primarily by the illicit drug-using activity of injecting drug users (IDUs) and by high-risk homosexual and heterosexual activity. Of the 213,641 diagnosed AIDS cases reported to the United States Centers for Disease Control (CDC), through February 1992, fully 90.4% derived from injecting drug use and high-risk sexual activity.

Yet vastly larger numbers of Americans are, today, HIV-infected and unaware of their predicament. Reliable data on the current number of asymptomatic HIV-positive Americans are unavailable; the most authoritative estimate places the number at 1.0 to 1.2 million as of late 1989. Due to the extraordinarily long incubation period for AIDS, HIV-infected persons take an average of eight to eleven years to develop symptoms of diagnosable AIDS. In the absence of a vaccine or curative antiviral therapy, once symptoms of AIDS are present, the disease is thought by many to be 100% fatal, although 51% of the San Francisco male cohort who seroconverted (became HIV-positive) from 1977–1980 were still alive eleven years later.

Contact tracing, the identification, location, and active recruitment of non-self-presenting persons likely to be exposed to communicable disease, has been a major public health practice in the United States since the syphilis control programs of the 1940s. Typically, once the source, asymptomatic patient is identified as a carrier of the disease, appropriate inquiry is made to identify the persons whose special relationships with the source patient place them in especially-acute risk of infection, such as sexual and needle-sharing partners. The at-risk partners are then personally contacted, notified of their risk of infection, and offered treatment or other intervention to reduce their risk of infection. Contact tracing, with mixed results, has been employed to combat epidemics of hepatitis B, chlamydia, and gonorrhea. The nature of the AIDS epidemic, however, creates extraordinary difficulties for contact tracing programs attempting to reduce the spread of HIV infection.

SPECIAL DIFFICULTIES IN CONTACT TRACING

The AIDS epidemic has distinctive features that vex contact tracing efforts.

Under-Diagnosed Nature of HIV Disease. Only a small fraction of HIV infection is currently being diagnosed in the United States. The most recent, official estimate of asymptomatic HIV-positive Americans is 1.0 to 1.2 million as of late 1989. But even this estimate is speculative; no rigorous, direct study of the number of unknowing HIV-positive Americans is currently available.

Moreover, the significance of under-reporting looms even larger in high-prevalence urban areas. New York City, for example, has 37,952 diagnosed AIDS cases, by the most recent report; vastly more than this number are HIV-positive. Such enormous numbers of HIV-positive persons in close circulation, themselves unaware of their disease and their ability to infect others, create gargantuan logistical burdens for any contact tracing program. The capacity of HIV-positive persons, unknowingly, to infect others is colossal.

Extremely Long Incubation Period Before Onset of AIDS Symptoms. The best current understanding is that the average incubation period, between HIV infection and the onset of symptoms supporting an AIDS diagnosis, is eight to eleven years. Even this number is soft, however, because 19% of the San Francisco male cohort were not only still alive but also were still asymptomatic, 11.1 years after their seroconversion to HIV-positivity, with no clinical signs or symptoms of HIV infection. Thus, the outside time duration of the HIV/AIDS incubation period has not yet been clinically established. It follows that each HIV-positive person has an average of at least eight to eleven years (and more) to infect others.

MULTIPLE SEX PARTNERS

High Mobility and Multiplicity of HIV-Risk Partners. Most high-risk transmitters of HIV infection tend to have many widely-dispersed, sex partners. In a 1991 study of drug use and sexual behaviors of the sex partners of IDUs, 24% of females and 40% of males had had sex with more than one partner in the prior six months. Likewise, CDC's 1992 study of the AIDS sexual risk-taking activity of American high-school students has concluded that more than half of all high-school students in America "engage in behaviors that place them at risk for AIDS"; 29% of American high-school students have had four or more sex partners by senior year. And in one of the few documented studies of HIV contact tracing programs to date, only two generations of contact tracing identified 83 at-risk sex contacts from a single HIV-positive source patient, and this in a rural, South Carolina community in only 24 months.

The logistical burden and expense of tracing and contacting

even two generations of sex partners from all of the presently-known HIV-infected persons in high-prevalence areas, like New York City, would be astounding—and probably would absorb the bulk of the entire current AIDS funding for such cities. Moreover, given the high mobility of HIV-infected IDUs and high-risk sexual partners, information discovered through contact tracing as to their location probably would not remain accurate for long; contact tracing information likely would remain current for only a small portion of any source patient's eight-to-eleven-year-plus period of infectivity.

PARTNER NOTIFICATION WOULD SAVE LIVES

Attempts to control the spread of AIDS have focused on such individualistic solutions as abstinence and safer sex. If everyone in the U.S. had practiced safer sex for the last ten years, partner notification might not be needed. But in the real world—where people postpone their mammograms and don't always buckle their seat belts, where people lie and conceal, where only about 13 percent of people in high-risk groups use condoms all the time—partner notification could surely save some lives.

Jane De Lynn, Glamour, August 1993.

Long Time Delay Between HIV Infection and the Ability to Detect the Infection. In the absence of any direct, clinical test for HIV, HIV infection can only be detected indirectly, by testing for the antibodies produced in reaction to HIV infection. The body produces these detectable antibodies only after a significant time delay after infection, which varies from six to twelve weeks or more. The source patient remains contagious for the delay period. Thus even the best contact tracing programs will fail to trace the at-risk needle-sharing and sexual partners of HIV-infected persons who have not yet seroconverted.

LACK OF CURE BLUNTS EFFECTIVENESS

Lack of Vaccine or Curative Antiviral Therapy. The present lack of an AIDS vaccine or curative antiviral therapy further blunts the effectiveness of contact tracing efforts. The voluntary citizen cooperation which is so necessary for effective contact tracing tends not to materialize, unless there is a widely-perceived benefit (such as a vaccine) that can justify so drastic an intrusion into the private lives of others. For example, contact tracing programs to combat the syphilis epidemic in the United States in the 1940s enjoyed the availability of a "magic bullet" remedy that would be dispensed to all at-risk persons traced by the program: penicillin. In contrast, the AIDS epidemic's absence of a "magic bullet" remedy has meant that little citizen participation will assist contact tracing efforts.

Importance of Maintaining Confidentiality. To an extent unprecedented in the history of epidemics, the AIDS epidemic coincided with a strong and pervasive societal demand for confidentiality. Confidentiality of HIV-positive identities has been justified on the ground of protecting source patients and their contacts from cruel discrimination and ostracism, leading to loss of employment, loss of insurance, or even vigilantism. Moreover, as a practical matter, confidentiality of HIV-positive patient information has been thought essential to achieve the voluntary cooperation required for public health interventions.

Reinforcing this, the lower federal courts have held that a constitutional right of privacy protects people known or suspected of having HIV disease. The 1977 decision of the United States Supreme Court in *Whalen v. Roe,* though not directly involving HIV or AIDS, has been interpreted broadly to support a general constitutional right to privacy of medical records, which requires both a limitation of access to public health officials who have a need to know, and also adequate protection of the confidentiality of record contents. An increasing number of court cases are upholding damage awards to compensate for violation of confidentiality concerning HIV-positivity. Similarly, the states which have enacted contact tracing legislation for HIV infection also have enacted laws specifically protecting the confidentiality of the HIV-positive case record and related information.

SPECIAL NEEDS FOR CONTACT TRACING

Given the many intrinsic difficulties of conducting contact tracing programs in the AIDS epidemic, it is inviting to reject such programs altogether. Yet the AIDS epidemic also presents a special need for contact tracing, in light of recent findings.

Sexual Partners and IDUs Generally Cannot Be Relied Upon to Notify Their At-Risk Partners of Their HIV Infection. In a recent, multi-site study of HIV-positive IDUs and their sexual partners, 19% either incorrectly reported their test results or incorrectly stated that they had not been tested at all. In another recent study, low-income Hispanic men who were HIV-positive and who knew of their seropositivity were studied to determine if they had told their sexual partners of their HIV status. An alarming 52% had kept their HIV infection secret from one or more sexual partners.

These alarming findings contradict earlier, general studies of

IDU self-report reliability, which had found fair agreement between self-reports and information shown in official records. However, these general studies were not in the AIDS context.

Notification of HIV-Positivity Helps Change AIDS-Risk Behaviors. The weight of the research to date is that notification of a person's HIV infection assists significantly in bringing about change in the person's high-risk AIDS behaviors. In a recent study of New York City blood donors who were notified they were HIV-positive, 60% significantly decreased their high-risk sexual behaviors after notification. Similarly, other researchers have found that notification of HIV-positivity is associated with significant decreases in high-risk behaviors, compared to persons who have tested HIV-negative or who have not been tested. The research on this point, however, is not unanimous.

Notification of HIV Infection Is Likely to Delay the Onset of AIDS Symptoms. Recent epidemiological research has shown that morphine, cocaine, and heroin speed the growth of HIV in cultures of human immune cells. If, as this research indicates, morphine, cocaine, and heroin are actual co-factors in the growth of HIV within the human immune system, the continued use of such drugs by IDUs after their HIV-positivity seriously exacerbates their HIV disease, and may well increase AIDS mortality and shorten the incubation period before AIDS symptoms.

STATE CONTACT TRACING PROGRAMS

The 39 states which by legislation have adopted some form of HIV contact tracing have addressed these special difficulties and special needs, in various ways.

Mandatory/Voluntary Disclosure of Known Contacts. Most contact tracing states have finessed the issue whether or not to mandate reporting and name notification of partner HIV-positive persons. They generally mandate contact tracing efforts by county or state public health officers (PHO) employed by official health departments, as long as the identities of at-risk partners already have been provided to the health department. Also, they usually mandate the reporting to the PHO, by physicians or testing laboratories, of non-identifying, epidemiological information on all persons who receive an HIV-positive test result. The majority of states, however, do not go further to mandate that physicians or other health care professionals notify third parties who are at risk of being HIV-infected by the source patient, even if the identities of at-risk partners are fully known and they are easily contacted. Ten states (AZ, CA, CT, IA, IL, MI, PA, NY, VA, WV) have gone so far as to declare there is no duty on the part of the physicians or health care providers to warn known at-risk partners.

CONFIDENTIALITY ISSUES

The contact tracing states generally have made great efforts to protect the confidentiality of HIV-positive source patient information. Five states (CT, LA, MI, NY, PA) require that the physician or PHO make the notification to at-risk partners "in person," or "face-to-face," unless circumstances reasonably prevent doing so. Fourteen states (AZ, CA, CT, FL, IL, IN, KY, LA, MD, MI, MT, NY, RI, WI) require the physician or PHO, prior to disclosure, to attempt through counseling to have the source patient notify his/her sexual and drug partners.

Fifteen states (AL, CA, CO, FL, GA, ID, IN, KS, MI, NH, NY, ND, RI, UT, WI) make unauthorized disclosure of HIV-positivity a crime (13 states, a misdemeanor; two states, ND and NH, a felony; the most serious category of crimes punishable by more than one year in prison). Thirteen states (AZ, DE, HI, IA, KY, LA, ME, MO, NJ, OR, VT, VA, WV) make unauthorized disclosure of HIV status a lesser, civil infraction, although punishable by monetary fines of up to $10,000 (HI, NJ).

Four states (CT, GA, LA, NY) require that the physician or PHO must specifically notify the HIV-positive source patient of his/her intent to notify the source patient's partner, prior to the notification. Two states (NY, LA) require that the source patient be given the option of having the disclosure of his/her HIV-positivity be made by a physician or a PHO, at the patient's choice. Ten states (CT, LA, NY, KS, SC, MT, NH, IN, WV, NJ) expressly mandate that specific identifying information of the source patient not be disclosed to the notified partners; partners are told only that there is reason to believe that a past or present sex or drug partner is HIV-positive. Twelve states (AZ, CA, FL, GA, IL, KS, KY, MO, OH, RI, TX, WV) specially authorize notification of spouses.

A DUTY TO WARN

Abrogation of Health Professionals' Common Law Duty to Warn Third-Parties in Danger. A striking feature of many of the state contact tracing programs for HIV infection is their nullification of the common law duty, traditionally placed upon physicians, psychiatrists, and similar health professionals, to warn known third-parties of a foreseeable danger to them from a patient. The classic illustration is provided by *Tarasoff v. Regents of University of California*, in which the California Supreme Court held that psychotherapists have an affirmative duty to warn a third-party of the foreseeable danger from their patients. The patient, during the course of therapy, had confided his intention to kill a third-party, but the psychotherapists did not contact the third-party to warn her, even though her identity and location had been disclosed by the patient. The patient in fact murdered her. The *Tarasoff* court ruled that, given the foreseeability of the danger, the severity of the harm to the third-party, and the ease by which the warning could have been made, the psychotherapists had had a common law duty to contact the third-party to warn her of the danger.

In this spirit, a long line of cases has held physicians to be under a duty to warn third-parties of specific risks to them from patients with smallpox, tuberculosis, syphilis, typhus, meningitis, scarlet fever, and diphtheria.

In stark contrast to this traditional common law duty, many of the contact tracing states have undercut their programs by granting extraordinary immunity from liability if health care professionals fail to contact known at-risk partners of HIV-infected patients. It is difficult to justify this grant of immunity on public health grounds. Ironically, it even contradicts the policy of the American Medical Association, which requires physicians as a matter of professional ethics to notify sexual and drug-sharing partners of their risk of HIV infection, if their infected patients refuse to do so.

Rather, physicians and similar health care professionals are the best-positioned to intervene effectively via contact tracing. Over half (52%) of all adults in the United States who were HIV-tested in 1988 received their testing through a physician. Moreover, they are the professionals who are most likely to learn the identities of at-risk partners of HIV-infected persons. It is a mistake to nullify their common law duty to warn.

NULLIFICATION OF DUTY

The special nature of the AIDS epidemic presents extraordinary difficulties for contact tracing programs in the United States attempting to reduce the spread of HIV infection. The 39 states which, by legislation, have created contact tracing programs, have deferred to the political exigencies as much as the epidemiological ones. They, to a significant extent, have de-emphasized compulsory notification of sexual and drug-sharing partners of HIV-positive persons, have emphasized anonymity of reporting, strongly have protected the confidentiality of HIV-positive patients and their sexual and drug-sharing partners, and have abrogated the common law duty to warn known, at-risk third-parties which the states have imposed upon physicians and other health care professionals for many generations. This general nullification of health care professionals' duty to warn known, easily-notified third-parties of foreseeable, life-threatening danger seems unwarranted in the AIDS context, cannot be justified on public health or patient-protection grounds, and undercuts the efficacy of the contact tracing programs of the states.

| "In studies during 1990, 60 percent of persons testing . . . stated that had their names been reported to the state, they would not have come in for testing."

PARTNER NOTIFICATION WOULD NOT REDUCE THE SPREAD OF AIDS

Mark S. Senak

Confidentiality laws and anonymous tests are necessary to protect those diagnosed with HIV/AIDS from discrimination and harassment, asserts Mark S. Senak in the following viewpoint. The use of contact tracing—the notification of sexual and needle-sharing partners of an HIV-positive person that they may have been exposed to the AIDS virus—would dissuade many people from being tested for HIV, Senak contends. Furthermore, he maintains, those states with large populations of HIV-positive residents do not have the resources to contact all the known partners. Senak is the planning director of AIDS Project Los Angeles and the author of *HIV, AIDS, and the Law*, from which this viewpoint is taken.

As you read, consider the following questions:

1. How does the *Tarasoff* case affect patient-physician confidentiality, in Senak's opinion?
2. Why are the groups most impacted by AIDS suspicious of large institutions, in the author's opinion?
3. What percentage of people polled say that they would use anonymous testing methods, as cited by Senak?

S tigma—the act of making someone different, of making an "other" out of a fellow human being—satisfies a vast array of needs for those who don't belong to the "other." This function is the very basis for discrimination. Acts of discrimination are one effect of stigma, while policies borne out of the creation of an "other" is another. There is an "other" if your skin is a different color; there is an "other" if you speak a different language or worship differently. Some legal theorists . . . find a basis for stigma in the way certain people might be perceived to be "polluting" on some level. That one is ill with disease appears to be yet another manifestation of "pollution" and therefore is a basis for stigma. The need to create stigma and cast some in the role of "other" begins with the majority's need to feel safe and secure from the perceived inroads of a minority. It is not this simple, though. The urge to stigmatize comes from a complicated variety of psychological and sociological causes. . . . But the fact is that it exists and we see it every day.

Given the issues rising from the stigma of disease, particularly with respect to people with HIV and those perceived to be at risk for HIV, the issue of confidentiality becomes one of paramount importance. No other disease in history has had the stigma attached to it that HIV disease has had, making confidentiality important not only for those affected, but for our entire public health-care system. As long as the powerful stigma is present, HIV medical treatment has to be confidential.

HIV EXCEPTIONALISM

With HIV disease, the combination of sex and drugs, transmission and mortality has heightened the air of blame that has often accompanied the experience of falling ill. The populations most affected by AIDS—gays, persons of color, and women—were already perceived as "other" in some capacity. Now, having HIV or being in a class of persons with a higher incidence of HIV burdens them with another layer of "other." A gay person of color who was tested positive for HIV has layer upon layer of circumstances that will, in the eyes of many, make him "other" and therefore subject to all kinds of discrimination.

Many public health experts feel that, in spite of stigma, HIV should be treated like any other illness or epidemic, often citing past victories or near-victories over diseases like syphilis or other sexually transmitted diseases. That model is based on finding those infected, identifying their contacts, and, meanwhile, intervening with education to prevent further infections and to cure.

But with HIV, the model breaks down at an obvious juncture.

There is, as yet, no cure. And the weight of stigma is greater than that which accompanies other sexually transmitted diseases.

Elizabeth Cooper, a public interest lawyer and professor at Brooklyn Law School, points to the flood of litigation that exists around HIV discrimination. "If you look to the numbers of discrimination cases that surround syphilis," she says, "and compare them to the numbers of cases involving HIV, there is just no comparison. With syphilis there are a few cases each year, while with HIV, there are hundreds."

Early in the epidemic, a public health doctrine evolved that divorced HIV from the traditional model for handling sexually transmitted disease. The doctrine is known as "HIV exceptionalism," a term first coined by Ronald Bayer in the *New England Journal of Medicine*.

HIV TESTS MUST STAY ANONYMOUS

The California Medical Association wants the names of people who test positive for the HIV virus to be reported and all of their sexual partners contacted.

On the face of it, this sounds reasonable. But it is not.

Proponents . . . argue that HIV/AIDS should be dealt with like any other sexually transmitted disease. But this scourge is different in two important respects. While most STDs [sexually transmitted diseases] can be cured, AIDS cannot. And an HIV diagnosis that becomes known too often invites discrimination that can leave a person without a job, a home or insurance.

Mark S. Senak, *Los Angeles Times*, March 13, 1995.

HIV exceptionalism is a reaction to the stigma of HIV and to the fact that the traditional model for sexually transmitted disease care does not work. It originated in the need to create an environment in which people could come forward for testing and feel somewhat safe. If stigma made testing unsafe, it was reasoned, HIV exceptionalism and the construction of laws of confidentiality could make it safe. The stigma could not be eliminated, but the effects of it could be deterred.

State legislatures around the nation, particularly in the epicenters of the AIDS epidemic, enacted laws providing for the confidentiality of people who stepped forward to take an HIV-antibody test. It became illegal in many jurisdictions to reveal to third parties that a person had tested antibody-positive. In addition, antidiscrimination legislation was also advanced, protecting people against discrimination as a result of being HIV-positive.

The entire construct of law, therefore, was in support of public health. The objective was to maintain a safe environment for people to be tested. If more people felt safe in coming forward for voluntary testing, then people who were infected would discover their status at an early stage of the HIV disease, preventing unknowing transmission to other parties. "When you assure an individual that his or her rights to privacy and confidentiality will be protected," says Liz Cooper, "you create a much more hospitable environment for someone to come in and take a risk and be tested."

Therefore, the entire public health strategy to beat the AIDS epidemic has been based on a new model, one that was an exception to the established rule for sexually transmitted diseases.

Cooper espouses the philosophy that public health principles and civil rights protections work in hand, not against one another: "When people portray issues around HIV as being protective of the public health versus protective of the civil rights of the individual, it is very upsetting. In fact, by protecting one, you automatically protect the other.". . .

THREE TYPES OF TESTING

There are basically three types of testing. The first, anonymous testing, is available in most states. Anonymous testing occurs at specifically designated sites. You go in for a blood test and your identity remains unknown throughout your entire transaction, even should you test positive. You are identified only by a number. In a week or two, you can go back and get the results of your test, usually, and in the best circumstances, accompanied by good quality face-to-face counseling. Anonymous testing offers many advantages. First and foremost, and most obvious, your identity is not revealed and no one has your name to share with an employer, a physician, a parent, a teacher, or, most important of all, an insurance company. Secondly, from society's point of view, anonymous testing sites attract the greatest number of persons who are likely to be HIV-positive. Thirdly, it would appear that the rate of testing generally increases when testing is offered anonymously. In southern Ontario, the rate of testing more than doubled when anonymous testing was introduced, indicating that anonymity may double the requests for testing. Lastly, at an anonymous test site, counseling is available.

There is a big difference between *anonymous testing* and *confidential testing*. The settings for confidential testing may vary. One might be a clinic specializing in the treatment of sexually transmitted diseases. It could be a community health center or special site set up solely for the purpose of providing an HIV test. Or, the setting could be your doctor's office. In some circumstances, if you are applying for a life insurance policy, it could even be at the behest of a life insurance company. It is important to remember, however, that whoever is testing you, confidential testing is not anonymous. The tester knows your name but promises not to reveal the results of your test to anyone. Confidential testing may, but does not always, involve counseling. There are exceptions to that rule that we will get to later.

The third way to be tested is without your consent or knowledge. Despite safeguards and laws that are designed to protect a person, this abuse nevertheless occurs. There are laws against murder, too, but it still happens. One should not suppose that testing will not occur simply because permission was not asked to perform a test. In Illinois, in 1994, a physician tested her patient for HIV over his own objections to being tested and then revealed the fact that the patient was HIV-positive to his sexual partner. In Maryland, a man sued the state because he was forced by officials to take an HIV test based on their belief that he was knowingly spreading HIV. . . .

EXCEPTIONS TO CONFIDENTIALITY

Because the ramifications of taking an HIV test are so vast and because there was the potential for so much abuse, legislators in high HIV-incidence states passed confidentiality legislation, prohibiting the disclosure of HIV test results to unauthorized persons.

However, with the enactment of confidentiality legislation, it became apparent that there needed to be exceptions to strict confidentiality. Medical personnel, for instance, need to exchange medical information about the patient in the course of treatment. Other circumstances have caused a tempering of the confidentiality statutes that were enacted early in the epidemic.

Today, many people argue that there are enough safeguards protecting people with AIDS against unfair treatment and discrimination, so confidentiality restrictions on HIV should be diminished or dissolved altogether in the interest of learning more about the epidemic and the people who are infected.

The earliest legislation in New York and California was fairly stringent, making it difficult, it was argued, for medical personnel to do their jobs. Confidentiality statutes were thereafter modified to allow medical personnel to exchange medical information that would include HIV status. Liz Cooper cites the fact that early in the epidemic people were afraid and that that fear motivated tough statutes: "People were afraid that this disease might ultimately affect them or their children and they were willing to be more protective than they might otherwise be." In addition, because AIDS was such an unknown factor, legislators tended to defer to physicians and their expertise in their recommendations.

However, there was a situation that caught public attention and became a lightning rod for moral indignation at the AIDS epidemic—the knowing and intentional infection of another person with HIV. This resulted not only in calls for the criminalization of HIV transmission but for a weakening of confidentiality statutes and the doctrine of HIV exceptionalism. One man in New York relayed a story of dating a woman for a three-month period, during which they had an active sex life. Suddenly, after three months, his partner called off the relationship. Her parting words were to tell him that he had better get tested for HIV because she had AIDS and she was determined to take as many men with her as she could. Just three days before that, the man had donated blood for his father's heart bypass surgery. An HIV-antibody test on that blood might be inconclusive, given the fact that there is a period of six weeks to six months before the body develops antibodies that will be detected in an HIV test. The man had very little recourse.

Because of the intentional transmission of HIV by some, confidentiality statutes were amended once again. Legislators wanted to address the fact that someone might be posing a threat and that the physician might be able to stop him or her. An exception to confidentiality was added to many confidentiality statutes to allow a physician to inform a third party of the impending danger posed by his patient if the doctor believed that the patient was not going to comply with safer needle-sharing or sex practices.

AN UNENVIABLE POSITION

The physician is in an extremely unenviable situation. Take, for example, the case of a physician who has a homosexual client who is deeply closeted, HIV-positive, and married. The physician counsels the patient on safer sexual practices and the patient explains that his wife is determined to have children and that therefore condoms are out of the question. Also out of the question is telling his wife about his true lifestyle. What is the physician to do?

Under most of the modified confidentiality statutes, a physician *may* inform the third party who is at risk but is not necessarily under an obligation to do so. Some statutes, as in New York and California, give the physician the option of informing the county health department, which in turn may inform the at-risk partner.

The statutory situation is complicated further by case law not even related to HIV/AIDS. In the 1980s, a man told his therapist that he intended to kill his girlfriend, a situation about which the therapist did nothing. Unfortunately, his client did do something; he went through with his threat and murdered his girlfriend. The family of the victim then sued the therapist for his failure to stop the murder. The therapist defended himself by citing the privilege that exists between a psychiatrist and his patient. In its ruling, the court, in what is called the *Tarasoff* case, ruled against the therapist, stating that the existence of a threat to an identified third party was sufficient cause to weaken the privileged relationship of doctor-patient.

What does *Tarasoff* mean to the practicing physician who is under a statutory duty of confidentiality vis-à-vis his patient but whose patient openly states an intention not to comply with safer sexual or needle-sharing practices? The answer is not immediately clear. The law passed by the legislature may say that the physician has the option, which he may or may not exercise, to inform the third party or, at the very least, the health department. On the other hand, case law may say that if the physician knows of impending harm to a third party because of the noncompliant behavior of his patient, he may in fact be liable in a civil suit if he does not relay this information.

MANDATORY NAMES REPORTING

While statutes were enacted to protect against unlawful disclosures of HIV status, many states also enacted requirements for physicians to report the names of those found to be infected with HIV. Epidemiologists argue that such reporting helps them understand where and among whom AIDS infections are occurring. Additionally, aside from the fact that the information provides a better demographical understanding of the epidemic and helps target prevention campaigns to the specific populations being infected, the information also allows them to conduct contact tracing, sometimes referred to as partner notification.

Contact tracing was already an element in the model of sexually transmitted disease intervention. In the context of AIDS, it means asking the infected person to voluntarily name his or her sexual or needle-sharing partners. Those people are then contacted by health officials, informed that they have been named as an intimate contact of a person infected with HIV and offered testing and counseling services. The two advantages of mandatory names reporting—the better understanding of the flow of the virus and the ability to perform contact tracing—convinced many states to adopt a names reporting policy.

In states where there is no mandatory names reporting for HIV, only AIDS cases are reported. This presents a different picture of the epidemic to epidemiologists, being that of persons who were infected long ago and only now have compromised immune systems. Mandatory names reporting of HIV infection, however, gives a picture of the epidemic that is closer in time to the point of infection.

For the most part, states requiring mandatory names reporting have been low HIV incidence states. Recently, however, higher-incidence states, such as New Jersey, have begun to join the ranks of those requiring names reporting. Mandatory names reporting necessarily raises the question of whether or not the reporting of names has a chilling effect on people coming forward for HIV testing, counseling, and care, diminishing the safety of the testing environment.

THE DISENFRANCHISED

In trying to answer the question, we must look at the populations most affected by HIV. To the greatest degree, as pointed out herein, the epidemic has impacted groups of people already disenfranchised: gay men and persons of color. The psychology and culture of these populations dictates that trust in large institutions does not reach as high a level as it may among other populations, such as white heterosexual men. In fact, large institutions have been notably oppressive to these populations. Two recent examples of this are the controversy surrounding the issue of gays in the military, where gays and lesbians have been the subject of accusations and discrimination, and California's passage of Proposition 187 in 1994. The latter is a ballot measure that states that health-care institutions shall refuse treatment to and, in fact, turn over the names of persons who are suspected of being in the country illegally. This measure turns health-care systems into immigration systems or systems akin to the criminal justice system.

In addition to being distrustful of large institutions, these populations have felt political winds shift considerably from election to election, as noted by the success of Proposition 187 and attempts to emulate it around the nation. Consider that in California there have been ballot initiatives over the years of the

AIDS epidemic that have sought quarantine of people with AIDS as well as mandatory names reporting. While those ballot initiatives ultimately failed at the polls, at the time they were presented on the ballot public opinion polls in California indicated that a majority of voters favored such measures. It was only after an expensive and extensive campaign that the measures were rejected, even in such conservative counties as Kern County in central California. In fact, the gay community had to divert time and resources from the care of people with AIDS to fight these initiatives. Given such events, why should disenfranchised populations affected by the epidemic trust the state with the names of persons who test positive for HIV? What is to be gained?

In fact, much might be lost by the presence of mandatory names reporting in high-incidence states. In studies during 1990, 60 percent of persons testing in one county in California anonymous testing sites stated that had their names been reported to the state, they would not have come in for testing. The heavy preference for privacy in testing is indicated as well in CDC [Centers for Disease Control and Prevention] studies, which demonstrate that Americans want more options for HIV testing. When asked if they intend to be tested under existing testing options, 8 percent of adults in 1992 indicated that they would seek testing in the coming year. But when asked if they would use anonymous home collection methods, the number jumped to 29 percent.

There is a very real danger that, given the psychology and culture of those affected by the epidemic, combined with the strong stigma that is still attached to having HIV infection, anonymous testing needs to be expanded and encouraged. Efforts such as mandatory names reporting stand to discourage testing by affected populations in exchange for information that is of dubious value. While contact tracing is a possible benefit, in high-incidence states the resources for contact tracing, a very labor intensive project, simply do not exist. In the final analysis, while over half the states now have mandatory names reporting, there is no evidence that the epidemic of HIV infection is under any better control in those states than in jurisdictions that do not report names.

PERIODICAL BIBLIOGRAPHY

The following articles have been selected to supplement the diverse views presented in this chapter. Addresses are provided for periodicals not indexed in the *Readers' Guide to Periodical Literature*, the *Alternative Press Index*, the *Social Sciences Index*, or the *Index to Legal Periodicals and Books*.

Ellen Wright Clayton	"Panel Comment: Why the Use of Anonymous Samples for Research Matters," *Journal of Law, Medicine & Ethics*, Winter 1995.
Christine Gorman	"Blood, Sweat, and Fears," *Time*, February 26, 1996.
Robin Marantz Henig	"The Lessons of Syphilis in the Age of AIDS," *Civilization*, November/December 1995. Available from 666 Pennsylvania Ave. SE, Suite 303, Washington, DC 20003.
Issues and Controversies On File	"HIV Testing," January 24, 1997. Available from Facts On File, 11 Penn Plaza, New York, NY 10001-2006.
Barbara J. Ledeen	"Sacrificing Babies on the Altar of Privacy," *Wall Street Journal*, August 3, 1995.
John Leo	"Babies Have Rights, Too," *U.S. News & World Report*, May 1, 1995.
Timothy F. Murphy	"The Ethics of HIV Testing by Physicians," *Journal of Medical Humanities*, Fall 1993. Available from 233 Spring St., New York, NY 10013-1578.
Wendy E. Parmet	"Panel Comment: Legislating Privacy: The HIV Experience," *Journal of Law, Medicine & Ethics*, Winter 1995.
Deidre Raver	"Rapists' Feminist Allies," *Women's Quarterly*, Autumn 1996. Available from 2111 Wilson Blvd., Suite 550, Arlington, VA 22201-3057.
Jeff Stryker	"Should the FDA Approve HIV Home Test Kits: Yes," *Priorities*, vol.7, no.3, 1995. Available from 1995 Broadway, 2nd Fl., New York, NY 10023-5860.
Sue Woodman	"The Push to Test Babies for HIV," *Ms.*, September/October 1994.

CHAPTER 3

How Can the Spread of AIDS Be Prevented?

Chapter Preface

The human immunodeficiency virus (HIV), widely acknowledged to be the cause of AIDS, is most commonly spread through the sharing of contaminated needles by intravenous drug users, semen during sexual intercourse, and from mother to child during pregnancy or delivery. Although the virus is often transmitted during homosexual sex between men, an increasing number of women are contracting HIV by means of heterosexual intercourse. In 1996, 40 percent of the women who were diagnosed with HIV were infected through heterosexual intercourse.

AIDS activists and researchers advocate the use of condoms as a prevention method, but condoms are not an option for many women whose male partners refuse to use them. However, women may soon have a new alternative to condoms—microbicides, chemical compounds that are inserted into the woman's vagina in the form of a gel or suppository. Microbicides have killed HIV, gonorrhea, chlamydia, herpes, and other sexually transmitted diseases in test tubes. One study found that the microbicide nonoxynol-9 was highly effective in preventing HIV transmission in women who used the agent every other day. Proponents of microbicides assert that the agents are the only prevention method that leaves the woman completely in control of protecting herself from HIV and other sexually transmitted diseases.

Microbicides do have their critics, however. Some contend that the availability of microbicides will encourage women to stop using condoms and other proven HIV prevention methods. Others cite a study of prostitutes who used twice the recommended dosage of nonoxynol-9; the high dosages apparently caused ulcerations in the vagina that could increase the likelihood of HIV infection.

Scientists are studying other types of microbicides as well, such as temperature-sensitive gels and compounds that prevent viral cells from attaching to vaginal cells. Most researchers agree that despite the microbicides' presumed efficacy against HIV transmission, other preventive measures should be used along with the microbicides to strengthen a woman's total protection. Some of these other methods for preventing HIV transmission are examined by the authors in the following chapter.

"The correct and consistent use of latex condoms during sexual intercourse . . . can greatly reduce a person's risk of acquiring or transmitting . . . HIV infection."

CONDOM USE CAN REDUCE THE SPREAD OF AIDS

Centers for Disease Control and Prevention

The Centers for Disease Control and Prevention (CDC) is a federal agency responsible for studying and monitoring infectious diseases. In the following viewpoint, the CDC argues that condoms are an effective means of preventing the transmission of the AIDS virus. When used correctly, condoms rarely break, the CDC maintains. Furthermore, the agency contends, sex education programs that include information on condoms do not lead to promiscuity among teenagers but do result in increased condom use among those teens who were already sexually active.

As you read, consider the following questions:

1. In the studies cited by the CDC, what percentage of partners in discordant couples who used condoms correctly and consistently contracted HIV?
2. What are the four myths concerning condom effectiveness, according to the CDC?
3. What are the advantages of plastic condoms over latex condoms, in the CDC's opinion?

From Facts About Condoms and Their Use in Preventing HIV Infection and Other STDs by the Centers for Disease Control and Prevention, HIV/AIDS Prevention Newsletter, February 1996.

With nearly 1 million Americans infected with HIV, most of them through sexual transmission, and an estimated 12 million cases of other sexually transmitted diseases (STDs) occurring each year in the United States, effective strategies for preventing these diseases are critical.

HIGHLY EFFECTIVE PROTECTION

Refraining from having sexual intercourse with an infected partner is the best way to prevent transmission of HIV and other STDs. But for those who have sexual intercourse, latex condoms are highly effective when used consistently and correctly.

The correct and consistent use of latex condoms during sexual intercourse—vaginal, anal, or oral—can greatly reduce a person's risk of acquiring or transmitting STDs, including HIV infection. In fact, *recent studies provide compelling evidence that latex condoms are highly effective in protecting against HIV infection when used for every act of intercourse.*

This protection is most evident from studies of couples in which one member is infected with HIV and the other is not, i.e., "discordant couples." In a 2-year study of discordant couples in Europe, among 124 couples who reported consistent use of latex condoms, none of the uninfected partners became infected. In contrast, among the 121 couples who used condoms inconsistently, 12 (10 percent) of the uninfected partners became infected.

In another study, among a group of 134 discordant couples who did not use condoms at all or did not use them consistently, 16 partners (12 percent) became infected. This contrasts markedly with infections occurring in only 3 partners (2 percent) of the 171 couples in this study who reported consistently using condoms over the 2-year period.

MYTHS ABOUT CONDOMS

Misinformation and misunderstanding persist about condom effectiveness. The Centers for Disease Control and Prevention (CDC) provides the following updated information to address some common myths about condoms. This information is based on findings from recent epidemiologic, laboratory, and clinical studies.

Myth #1: *Condoms don't work.* Some persons have expressed concern about studies that report failure rates among couples using condoms for pregnancy prevention. Analysis of these studies indicates that the large range of efficacy rates is related to incorrect or inconsistent use. In fact, latex condoms are highly effective for pregnancy prevention, but only when they are used properly. Research indicates that only 30 to 60 percent of men who claim to use condoms for contraception actually use them for every act of intercourse. Further, even people who use condoms every time may not use them correctly. Incorrect use contributes to the possibility that the condom could leak at the base or break.

THE ONLY WAY OF ENSURING PROTECTION

[In the early years of the AIDS epidemic], some health departments sought to promote condom use because it was the only way of ensuring self-protection. In an AIDS-prevention advertisement produced by the New York City Health Department, in the style of pop art, a man and woman are shown embracing and thinking, "I hope he [she] doesn't have AIDS!" To this, the voice of the Health Department responds, "You can't live on hope." The text of the advertisement continues:

> You hope this guy is finally the right guy.
> You hope this time she just might be the right one.
> And you both hope the other one is not infected with the AIDS virus.
> Of course, you could ask. But your partner might not know.
> That's because it's possible to carry the AIDS virus for many years without showing any symptoms.
> The only way to prevent getting infected is to protect yourself. Start using condoms.
> Every time. Ask him to use them. If he says no, so can you.

Ronald Bayer, *New England Journal of Medicine*, June 6, 1996.

Myth #2: *Condoms frequently break.* Some have questioned the quality of latex condoms. Condoms are classified as medical devices and are regulated by the Food and Drug Administration (FDA). Every latex condom manufactured in the United States is tested for defects before it is packaged. During the manufacturing process, condoms are double-dipped in latex and undergo stringent quality control procedures. Several studies clearly show that condom breakage rates in this country are less than 2 percent. Most of the breakage is likely due to incorrect usage rather than poor condom quality. Using oil-based lubricants can weaken latex, causing the condom to break. In addition, condoms can be weakened by exposure to heat or sunlight or by age, or they can be torn by teeth or fingernails.

Myth #3: *HIV can pass through condoms.* A commonly held misperception is that latex condoms contain "holes" that allow passage of HIV. Laboratory studies show that intact latex condoms provide a highly effective barrier to sperm and microorganisms, including HIV and the much smaller hepatitis B virus.

Myth #4: Education about condom efficacy promotes sexual activity. Five U.S. studies of specific sex education programs have demonstrated that HIV education and sex education which included condom information either had no effect upon the initiation of intercourse or resulted in delayed onset of intercourse; four studies of specific programs found that HIV/sex education did not increase frequency of intercourse, and a program that included resistance skills actually resulted in a decrease in the number of youth who initiated sex. In addition, a World Health Organization (WHO) review cited 19 studies of sex education programs that found no evidence that sex education leads to earlier or increased sexual activity in young people. In fact, five of the studies cited by WHO showed that such programs can lead to a delay or decrease in sexual activity.

In a recent study of youth in Switzerland, an AIDS prevention program focusing on condom use did not increase sexual activity or the number of sex partners. But condom use did increase among those who were already sexually active. A 1987 study of young U.S. men who were sent a pamphlet discussing STDs with an offer of free condoms did not find any increase in the youths' reported sexual activity.

OTHER HIV PREVENTION STRATEGIES

Condoms for Women. The female condom or vaginal pouch has recently become available in the United States. A small study of this condom as a contraceptive indicates a failure rate of 21–26 percent in 1 year among typical users; for those who use the female condom correctly and consistently, the rate was approximately 5 percent. Although laboratory studies indicate that the device serves as a mechanical barrier to viruses, further clinical research is necessary to determine its effectiveness in preventing transmission of HIV. If a male condom cannot be used, consider using a female condom.

Plastic Condoms. A polyurethane male condom was approved by FDA in 1991 and is now available in the United States. It is made of the same type of plastic as the female condom. The lab studies show that the new polyurethane condoms have the same barrier qualities as latex. Lab testing has shown that particles as small as sperm and HIV cannot pass through this polyurethane material. A study of the effectiveness of this polyurethane condom for prevention of pregnancy and STDs is underway. The new polyurethane condoms offer an alternative for condom users who are allergic to latex. Also, polyurethane condoms can be made thinner than latex, have no odor, and are safe for use with oil-based lubricants.

Spermicides. Although studies indicate that nonoxynol-9, a spermicide, inactivates HIV in laboratory testing, it is not clear whether spermicides used alone or with condoms during intercourse provide protection against HIV. Therefore, latex condoms with or without spermicides should be used to prevent sexual transmission of HIV.

MAKING RESPONSIBLE CHOICES

In summary, sexually transmitted diseases, including HIV infection, are preventable. The effectiveness of responsible prevention strategies depends largely on the individual. Whatever strategy one chooses, its effectiveness will depend primarily on consistent adherence to that choice.

"Promotion of condom usage will only abet and increase the spread of AIDS around the globe."

CONDOM USE WILL INCREASE THE SPREAD OF AIDS

Anthony Zimmerman

Promotion of condom usage to prevent HIV infection is a short-term solution, argues Anthony Zimmerman in the following viewpoint. Zimmerman contends that in the long run, encouraging condom use will actually increase the spread of AIDS because condoms encourage promiscuity, especially among teenagers, and because condoms are not a reliable barrier against HIV infection. Even if they use a condom, promiscuous teens have a high chance of contracting sexually transmitted diseases, including HIV, he maintains. Zimmerman is a Catholic priest and a frequent contributor to *Fidelity*, a monthly Catholic magazine.

As you read, consider the following questions:
1. What percentage of condom usage prevents HIV infection, according to the World Health Organization study cited by Zimmerman?
2. What two reasons does the author give to support his contention that condom usage will increase the spread of AIDS?
3. In Zimmerman's opinion, what will lead to the extinction of AIDS?

From Anthony Zimmerman, "The Coming Population Explosion," *Fidelity*, April 1994. Reprinted by permission of *CultureWars*, 206 Marquette Ave., South Bend, IN 46617.

I f the question is asked whether the promotion of the use of condoms serves to prevent AIDS, or to boost AIDS, the answer is likely to be: it may brake its spread in the short run; but accelerates its spread in the long run.

ONLY SIXTY PERCENT EFFECTIVE

If condoms are recommended to people who already are promiscuous, then, yes, condoms may decelerate the spread of AIDS among such a population, but not for long. According to Population Reports:

> An overall estimate can be drawn from a recent analysis for the World Health Organization (WHO), combining data from nine published studies. This analysis found that condom users face a risk about two-thirds that of non users of developing gonorrhea, trichomoniasis, or chlamydial infection. Condoms offer less protection against STDs, such as herpes simplex, that can cause lesions in places not covered by condoms. . . . Combining data from 10 studies of HIV transmission, the same analysis found a relative risk of about 0.4 for condom users—less than half as great a risk as for non users. Just as in family planning studies, many of the participants in these studies did not use the condom consistently or, in some cases, correctly.

The figures of this WHO study provide small comfort: if condom usage prevents infection only sixty percent compared with non-usage, then it is but a matter of time and multiple intercourses until all condom users—one hundred percent—are infected. It is like putting only four bullets into the Russian roulette pistol with ten receptors, and then pointing the pistol to one's brain and pulling the trigger continuously until death strikes.

CONDOMS INCREASE PROMISCUITY

But in the long run promotion of condom usage will only abet and increase the spread of AIDS around the globe, and this for two reasons: 1) Promotion of the condom by those in authority—school teachers, health workers, government agents—tends to increase sexual promiscuity in a population which is not promiscuous, and that includes the majority of adolescents in the world before they achieve sexual maturity. Adolescents are not yet promiscuous during sexual latency. But when those in authority mis-educate them to use the condom, and so break down the natural and cultural barriers against use of sex before marriage, juvenile promiscuity tends to increase geometrically and to completely overwhelm the weak braking action of condoms against AIDS infection. 2) Promotion of the condom and its increased usage induces a false sense of security and pseudo-responsibility, which again tends to multiply sexual encounters beyond the rate it would have in the absence of condom promotion. Herbert Ratner, a pediatrician and editor of *Child and Family*, maintains:

> Those who stress condom usage only put the seal of approval on active genital sex. . . . The advocates of the condom seduce our young people into deep waters from which they seldom emerge. Its intensive promotion does more to arouse and stimulate the imagination and encourage genital sex among the young than to curb unprotected sex among the promiscuous.

Reprinted by permission of Chuck Asay and Creators Syndicate.

Dispensing condoms from the school will eliminate many of the reasons for teenage restraint and confuse the vital moral message about morality. Distributing condoms in school will therefore cause more teenage promiscuity and more, not fewer STDs including AIDS. "Distribute condoms in school, and you weaken reasons for kids not to have sex," writes Dr. Paul Cameron, a professional researcher of the spread of AIDS.

AIDS IN THE FUTURE
Fingers will be pointed in the future at those who seduced our youth today by dispensing condoms in schools to the children. As of now, the prevalent HIV virus in the USA is the type which

spreads more easily through sodomitic intercourse among homosexual practitioners, than the African types which spread through heterosexual intercourse. For example, in Washington, D.C., seventy-nine percent of the AIDS cases were among the homosexuals; by 1991 about 5,500 homosexuals had been infected and 1,705 had died. Read: the ghetto of sodomites is going into extinction, and that could lead to the extinction of AIDS.

However, because Planned Parenthood and like-minded promoters of condom usage among school children instigate heterosexual promiscuity among the boys and girls attending schools, a shadow of death already menaces the gates of our schools: the next wave of a mutated HIV virus which spreads easily by heterosexual contact may strike our schools like the atom bombs which devastated Nagasaki and Hiroshima. It will be small comfort for survivors to point fingers at that time and say: "I told you so!" The time to check promotion of condoms in schools, and so to prevent massive death of our youth from AIDS in the future, is now. The time to circle the wagons in parishes, schools, towns and cities is now.

THE NEW BLACK DEATH

If worse comes to worse—if the HIV subtypes which spread via heterosexual intercourse infect our youth in schools where sex education now promotes promiscuity—we will face a situation not unlike that of the apocalyptic black death which devastated Europe and re-wrote its history in the 14th century. *Encyclopedia Britannica*'s entry on the plague reads, "The number of deaths was enormous, reaching in various parts of Europe two-thirds or three-fourths of the population." What happens now in some villages of Uganda [some of which have three to four funerals per week or have become ghost towns], would become commonplace in cities and towns of the USA where youth has become promiscuous thanks to sex mis-education. The promotion of condoms would perhaps decelerate the first great assault of the epidemic, but only serve to generate total destructive power in the end.

| "[It is] time for young people to understand that a deadly epidemic is afoot and . . . it can kill even them."

AIDS Prevention Programs for Teenagers Should Emphasize Safe Sex

Linda Ellerbee

In the following viewpoint, Linda Ellerbee maintains that teenagers are especially vulnerable to contracting HIV because of their belief in their immortality. This belief is typical in young people, Ellerbee asserts, and often leads them to ignore safety precautions. Therefore, she contends, education and prevention programs should target teenagers and should stress the use of condoms to prevent HIV infection. Ellerbee is a nationally syndicated columnist.

As you read, consider the following questions:

1. In Ellerbee's opinion, how does the availability of other means of birth control affect teens' condom usage?
2. What percentage of teenagers have had sexual intercourse, according to the Centers for Disease Control and Prevention study, as cited by Ellerbee?

From Linda Ellerbee, "Remembering Immortality," *Liberal Opinion Week*, June 21, 1993. Reprinted by permission of the author.

In an issue of News of the Weird, a strange and wonderful newsletter chronicling that which is improbable but accurate, I read a story about a man named Merlyn Starley, an industrial chemist who lives in San Francisco. In October of 1992, Mr. Starley applied for and was granted a patent for condoms with suspenders. Mr. Starley's invention, which consists of two plastic clips and an adhesive attached to the wearer's leg, is supposed to prevent the condom from slipping off while being used.

Now think hard for a minute. I want you to imagine your basic 18-year-old, at-risk teenager, caught in a lively moment, all glands pumping, pausing to put on his suspenders, too. Do you have trouble imagining that?

Right.

Pretty silly, the idea of getting young people to wear those things when we aren't doing a very good job getting young people to wear regular condoms. Not even to save their lives.

Living Forever

According to a 1993 study by the Centers for Disease Control, nearly half of sexually active high school students say they use condoms for birth control, but many fail to use them to prevent AIDS when other means of birth control are available. In other words, if the girl is using birth control pills, the boy probably isn't using a condom. Never mind that birth control pills do not protect anybody against AIDS.

Either young people don't know this very useful piece of information, or they don't care.

My guess is that a lot of it is the latter. The young don't care. They don't care because they're young; they know they're going to live forever. I remember when I knew I was. A great feeling. Death so far down the road it might as well not exist. Hey!—maybe it doesn't!

Yeah. I remember.

None of this means the young are stupid. They're not; they're only young—and often ignorant (except for those who are, in fact, stupid, which is unfixable, anyway). How wonderful it would be to live in a world in which it were not so incredibly dangerous for them to retain their ignorance. As fortune would have it, such is not the case.

Facts remain facts. AIDS is killing teenagers. Teenagers are having sex. The Centers for Disease Control's high school survey, based on a questionnaire given to 12,272 students at 137 schools in the United States, found a very high degree of sexual activity among teenagers. Fifty-four percent said they had had intercourse, and that rose to two-thirds for the seniors.

TIME FOR A NEW MESSAGE

Yet for 12 years, our elected government did its best to pretend young people in America simply were not "doing it," or that if they were, they could be easily persuaded to stop. Abstention was the only message being sent.

Quite obviously, it was not received.

Time now to send some new messages. Time for young people to understand that a deadly epidemic is afoot and, impossible as it may seem, it can kill even them. Time for young people to understand the value of condoms in preventing disease.

KNOWLEDGE IS NOT HARMFUL

Abstaining from any risky activity is always an option. But when it's your only message, you haven't educated. And you risk not reaching those who are most vulnerable. . . .

By the time children are faced with decisions about sex and drugs, they should know enough about H.I.V. and AIDS to consider the risks of transmission.

Edward McCabe, New York Times, May 30, 1994.

Time for our government to start talking sense when it comes to sex. Time for our government to start making sense when it comes to sex.

Consider this.

In 1991, the U.S. Agency for International Development shipped 200 million condoms to Pakistan to help fight AIDS. A year later it announced it would halt shipments because of questions about Pakistan's nuclear weapons program.

Try for a moment to follow the thought process here. I can't.

Nor do I understand why we were willing to hand out condoms to save the lives of Pakistani young at a time when our own young were being told to just say no. Either some politicians also believe the young are immortal, or they don't much care. My advice to the young is to pay close attention to the advice of 20th-century philosopher Bruce Springsteen, who so eloquently said it for all of us.

"Blind faith in your leaders," said Mr. Springsteen, "can get you killed."

4

> "Sexual abstinence is the only known 100 percent effective method of preventing unintended pregnancy and HIV transmission."

AIDS Prevention Programs for Teenagers Should Emphasize Abstinence

New York Bishops

The following viewpoint is excerpted from a statement issued by the bishops of New York State objecting to the distribution of condoms in public schools. School programs that promote condom usage to prevent the spread of AIDS are irresponsible, the bishops maintain, because they encourage meaningless sex and teach teenagers to be promiscuous. The bishops also assert that abstinence is the only completely effective way to prevent both pregnancy and HIV infection. School officials should therefore require AIDS education programs to stress abstinence, the authors conclude.

As you read, consider the following questions:

1. In the authors' opinion, what message do condom distribution programs send to teenagers?
2. What has been the effect of abstinence programs such as Project Respect on the pregnancy rates of high school students, according to the authors?
3. In the bishops' opinion, how can schools help alleviate the AIDS crisis?

Excerpted from the New York Bishops' "Statement on Public Schools' Condom Distribution" as it appeared in the January 21, 1993, issue of *Origins*. (Endnotes in the original have been deleted here.)

To our fellow citizens in New York state,

Today, our nation's attention is focused on the great tragedy of AIDS. Each day we continue to lose our sons and daughters, brothers and sisters, neighbors and friends to this deadly disease.

The insidious way in which AIDS devastates individuals and ends human life stirs in us a deep compassion for those infected, those at risk of infection and our society as a whole. Our concern compels a response steeped in nothing less than deliberate, prayerful thinking directed toward wholeness, health, moral values and the healing of our society.

CONDOMS IN SCHOOL

Today, New York City public high schools distribute free condoms to students on request, and other school districts throughout our state consider similar plans. Drugstores, grocery markets and gift shops boldly promote the illusion of "safe sex" through condom sales. Each day rock music sells sex without responsibility, and television uses sex to sell everything from blue jeans to automobiles.

As moral leaders, we bishops of New York state object to the distribution of condoms in public schools as an irresponsible education policy in responding to the AIDS crisis. Such an approach fails to respect the human dignity of young people and depreciates the life-giving gift of human sexuality. It also undermines the primary right of parents to guide and rear their children.

As teachers, we also strongly object to school condom distribution on practical grounds, and, based on our review of the literature and scholarly research, seriously question the effectiveness of such programs.

Therefore, as teachers, as pastors and friends, we share our concerns with you, the people of New York state.

CONDOMS ARE NOT THE ANSWER

We firmly believe, on both moral and practical grounds, that distributing condoms to young people is not the proper approach to the AIDS epidemic. It is just one more example of society's quick-fix, Band-Aid approach to problems. To help our youth understand issues of human sexuality, we must look deeper and work harder to send the right message. The right message is that human sexuality is beautiful, powerful, sacred and good. It is a gift of God that must be used responsibly and morally.

As church leaders, we are not unaware of the activities in which some adolescents may be engaged. We know that some are involved in sexual activity; others are drinking alcohol, using crack and guns. In the latter instances, society does not hesitate to tell them, "There is a better way. You should not engage in these activities." We would think it ludicrous to distribute free beer or drugs or guns in schools! Yet we willingly offer a false sense of security to children in the form of condoms, thereby encouraging and tacitly approving dangerous sexual activity.

The message such programs send to young people is, "We have no faith in you." They tell adolescents that we've given up, sold out and assume they will do wrong. It signals total disregard for the dignity of our young people by suggesting they are incapable of moral behavior consistent with their Judeo-Christian ethic. Have we deemed our youth hopelessly beneath our expectations and challenge?

At a time of adolescent uncertainty, sexual maturation and unparalleled questioning, we should be offering young people clear guidance and strong direction. We should be giving them a message of hope, faith, self-worth and self-respect. We believe in the dignity of our young. We believe that with proper guidance, with parental involvement and with programs built upon the concept of deepening self-esteem, our youth will respond to the message to live their lives consistent with healthy sexual attitudes and the values that encourage sexual abstinence.

There is a better way.

MORAL DIMENSIONS

Our sexuality is a gift from God. Sexual intercourse is the most intimate and beautiful act of love between two married people. Imagine! Two people can come together whose love is so great, so powerful, that the physical and emotional bonding of that love has the capability of producing another human being!

We should be teaching our children reverence and awe for such an act; it reflects the total commitment shared by a husband and wife. It is a totally selfless, unconditional love which is expressed in sexual intercourse, a sign of the fidelity, acceptance, commitment and closeness shared by married lovers. We must give our children the understanding that the more powerful the gift, the more cautious and responsible we must be in using it.

The emotional bonding which occurs in physical genital activity between two persons may not be fully understood by those who promote condoms for teen-agers. Teens who engage in premarital sexual activity feel this bonding, too, and are often deeply hurt when the casual, uncommitted relationship ends. Feelings of emptiness, loss and guilt are not uncommon when one gives of oneself totally to another, only to be tossed aside for a new "steady."

Children experience extremely rapid emotional, physical, social, psychological and spiritual growth during their adolescent years. Our culture encourages sexual activity for young people as a solution to their needs, doubts, desires and questions. But our children do not need to be set up for an emotional trauma through early sexual activity. Casual, premarital sex cheapens sex. Young people need to hear that there is a better way, that responsible and meaningful sex involves love, commitment and respect. . . .

AN ALTERNATIVE TO CONDOMS

As a church, we firmly believe that we must discuss sex openly and honestly with children, answering all of their questions. Several of our dioceses have instituted human sexuality curricula in their Catholic schools and religious education programs. These comprehensive programs reflect sound scientific and psychological information, the teachings of the church and a clear understanding of the challenges facing adolescents today. They emphasize the value of each individual person, the gift of sexuality, parental involvement and the importance of family.

There are other programs, not specifically church affiliated, which teach the value of chastity and the positive, healthy outcomes of refraining from premarital sexual activity. Project Respect, based in Illinois, has recently demonstrated a 45 percent lower pregnancy rate among high school sophomores and juniors using the "Sex Respect" curricula. Fertility Appreciation for Families, a program which promotes abstinence, respect for life, moral values and discussion with parents, recently found pregnancy rates among the 15–19 year-old participants to be 95 percent lower than the national norm.

Why then do we shun abstinence programs or glibly respond that they have been tried and found wanting, when in fact they are working? We believe that hoping for abstinence while simultaneously encouraging the illusion of "safe sex" through condom use simply does not and will not work.

Sexual abstinence is the only known 100 percent effective method of preventing unintended pregnancy and HIV transmission. New York state education regulations recognize this and rightly require that AIDS instruction in schools must "stress abstinence as the most appropriate and effective premarital protection against AIDS."

All schools in the state, including Catholic schools, are required to educate our young people to the nature and cause of this deadly disease. It is critical that children and young adults, as well as adults, know the truth about HIV and the AIDS disease.

It is also vital that schools be encouraged to do their job of imparting basic knowledge and skills in living. Schools can help to alleviate the AIDS crisis by teaching responsible habits of thinking and living, discipline and moral values. They can encourage young people to become involved in meaningful job preparation, athletic and creative activities.

Parental Authority and Family Unity

The standards for adolescents growing up in today's society should be set by the family and reinforced by the school. Parents are, and always have been, the primary educators of their children. Having conferred life on them in God's presence, they have the right and responsibility to guide the growth and development of their sons and daughters and to instill in them the values they wish to inculcate.

David Hitch. Reprinted with special permission of King Features Syndicate.

We urge parents, parent surrogates, guardians, teachers and adult relatives to challenge young people to live self-respecting moral lives and to say no to every moral evil which harms their dignity, their bodies, their minds and souls. We urge parents to show their children that they care about them, to turn off the television and spend some quality time with them. We urge them to demonstrate to their children by their actions that family is an important value.

Tragically, we recognize that an increasing number of New York's children now live without any parental supervision from a mother or a father. These young people, many of whom are scarred by years of abuse and neglect, and growing up in inner cities alongside drugs, AIDS and guns, deserve our special love and concern. All adult role models, guardians and persons in "parental" relationships to these children should be sensitive, compassionate and consistent in conveying the message that the children are unique, precious individuals and that sexual activity is sacred.

We urge parents, guardians, teachers and all adults to lead by example as loving, moral, chaste people. And we encourage them to inspire our young people to new heights and challenge them to be the best that they can be.

A TIME TO SPEAK THE TRUTH

We are confronted with a disease that kills. This is not the time for rhetoric or lame excuses. It is not the time to take the easy way out. It is time to speak the truth.

We call upon all those involved in policy making and program implementation in the education and health care fields to do all within their power to discourage the quick-fix "solution" of condom distribution and to promote sexual abstinence as a healthy lifestyle for our young people. We bishops stand ready to work with you in this important task.

We call upon parents, guardians, teachers, counselors, advertisers and all those involved in education and health care agencies in our state to speak the truth, to speak it loudly and clearly and continuously, because our young people can live with nothing less.

"Needle exchange programs are based on a sound public health principle—eliminating the item that helps transmit infection from one person to another."

NEEDLE EXCHANGE PROGRAMS CAN CONTROL THE SPREAD OF AIDS

Peter Lurie and Pamela DeCarlo

HIV is known to be transmitted through blood, and injection drug users are at risk of infection if they share contaminated needles. In the following viewpoint, Peter Lurie and Pamela De-Carlo maintain that needle exchange programs (NEPs), which distribute sterile needles in exchange for used ones, are an effective means of controlling the spread of HIV. According to the authors, NEPs frequently offer other services to help drug users get off drugs and into treatment. Studies show that NEPs do not encourage drug use, they assert. Lurie is a physician and AIDS researcher at the Public Citizen's Health Research Group and an assistant professor with the University of California San Francisco's Center for AIDS Prevention Studies. DeCarlo is also an AIDS researcher at UCSF.

As you read, consider the following questions:

1. According to Lurie and DeCarlo, why do drug users share needles?
2. Why are needles and syringes difficult for drug users to obtain, according to the authors?
3. What evidence do the authors present to support their contention that needle exchange programs are cost-effective?

From Peter Lurie and Pamela DeCarlo, "Does Needle Exchange Work?" HIV Prevention: Looking Back, Looking Ahead, February 1995. Reprinted by permission of the Center for AIDS Prevention Studies (CAPS), San Francisco.

Why do we need needle exchange? More than a million people in the United States inject drugs, at a cost to society (in health care, lost productivity, accidents, and crime) of more than $50 billion a year. People who inject drugs imperil their health. If they contract HIV, their needle-sharing partners, sexual partners and offspring may also be endangered.

One-third of all AIDS cases are linked to injection drug use. For women, 64% of all AIDS cases are due to injection drug use or sex with partners who inject drugs. Injection drug use is the source of infection for more than half of all children born with HIV.

Around the world and in more than sixty locations in the United States, needle exchange programs have sprung up to address drug injection risks. These programs not only distribute clean needles and safely dispose of used ones for injection drug users (IDUs), they generally offer a variety of related services, including referrals to drug treatment and HIV counseling and testing.

STERILE NEEDLES ARE UNAVAILABLE

Why do drug users share needles? In part because there are not enough needles and syringes to go around. The overwhelming majority of IDUs are aware of the risk of the transmission of HIV and other diseases if they share contaminated equipment. However, sterile needles are not always available or affordable.

Most US states have paraphernalia laws that make it a crime to possess or distribute drug paraphernalia not for a "legitimate medical purpose," which subjects drug injectors to prosecution. In addition, ten states and the District of Columbia have laws that require a prescription to buy a needle and syringe. Even where over-the-counter sales of syringes are permitted by law, pharmacists are often unwilling to sell to IDUs.

In July of 1992, the state of Connecticut passed a law permitting the purchase and possession of up to ten syringes without a prescription. After the new law went into effect, the sharing of needles among IDUs decreased, and there was a shift from street needle and syringe purchasing to pharmacy purchasing.

How can injection risks be reduced? Getting drug injectors into treatment and off drugs is the best answer. Unfortunately, not all drug injectors are ready to quit. Even those who are highly motivated may find few services available. Drug treatment centers frequently have long waiting lists and fewer than 15% of IDUs are in treatment at any given time.

For those who cannot or will not stop injecting drugs, the best way to avoid spreading HIV is to use a sterile needle for each injection, or at least not to share needles. Users who share should disinfect their injection equipment thoroughly with bleach, although this is not as safe as always using a sterile needle and syringe.

CUTTING THE RISK

- Number of injection drug users in U.S. large metropolitan areas: 1,460,300
- Number HIV positive: 204,000 or 14%
- Estimated new HIV infections among injection drug users: 19,000/year
- HIV infections potentially averted through implementing needle-exchange programs:
  1987 to 1995 4,394–9,666
  1996 to 2000 5,150–11,329

Peter Lurie and Ernest Drucker, *Wall Street Journal*, July 10, 1996.

Does needle exchange encourage drug use? There is no evidence that needle exchange programs increase the amount of drug use by needle exchange clients or in the wider community. A study of a San Francisco needle exchange program that opened in 1988 found that from 1987 to 1992, frequency of injecting drugs among street-recruited IDUs declined from 1.9 to 0.7 injections per day. The mean age of IDUs increased from 36 to 42 years, and the percentage of new initiates into injection drug use dropped from 3% to 1%. Drug abuse and the recruitment of new or younger users did not increase in the presence of the exchange; in fact, the exchange may have helped *decrease* the amount of drug abuse in the area.

REDUCING THE RATE OF HIV INFECTION

Does needle exchange reduce the spread of HIV? Yes, almost certainly. Needle exchange programs are based on a sound public health principle—eliminating the item that helps transmit infection from one person to another, just as reducing the number of mosquitoes helps prevent malaria.

In New Haven, Connecticut, a study tested needles returned to the needle exchange, and developed a mathematical model that estimated a possible 33% reduction in the rate of new HIV infections among needle exchange program clients. A review of the modeling literature by a CDC-sponsored research team suggested this estimate may even be low.

In New York City, New York, a large comprehensive study of needle exchange programs found that the rate of new HIV infections for participants in the exchange was 2%. This rate is much lower than the estimated 4–7% HIV infection rate among IDUs not enrolled in the exchange. The study also found that among clients, using rented syringes decreased 75%, using borrowed syringes decreased 62%, and using alcohol wipes before injecting went up 150%.

Needle exchange programs have also achieved reductions in the rate of hepatitis B infection, which can also be spread through sharing needles. In Tacoma, Washington, clients of a needle exchange program were up to eight times less likely to contract hepatitis B and C than non-client IDUs.

Needle exchange programs also have the potential to act as a bridge to drug treatment, and can provide referrals and, in some cases, actual services for HIV testing and counseling, primary medical care, tuberculosis and sexually transmitted disease screening. In Seattle, Washington, the needle exchange program issued 181 vouchers for drug treatment, and 78% were successfully redeemed. Fifty-eight percent entered methadone maintenance, and 86% of those were still in treatment three months after intake.

Is needle exchange cost-effective? Yes. The median annual budget for running a program is $169,000, with a range of $31,000–$393,000. This translates to $.71 to $1.63 per syringe distributed. In addition, mathematical models predict that over five years, needle exchanges could prevent many HIV infections among clients, their sex partners, and offspring, at a cost of about $9,400 per infection averted. This is far below the $119,000 lifetime cost of treating an HIV-infected person.

PART OF A BROADER STRATEGY

What must be done? Efforts to increase the availability of sterile needles must be a part of a broader strategy of drug treatment and prevention efforts. The currently available data provide sufficient evidence to repeal the ban on the use of federal funds for needle exchange services. States with prescription laws should repeal them; those with paraphernalia laws should revise them insofar as they restrict access to needles and syringes. Local governments and public health officials should work with community groups to develop comprehensive approaches to HIV prevention among IDUs and their sexual partners, including, but certainly not limited to, needle exchange programs.

Needle exchange programs have become a standard of public health practice around the world. Failure to support ready access to sterile needles has been described as tantamount to medical malpractice.

| "There is no empirical evidence to suggest that lives will be saved through needle exchanges."

NEEDLE EXCHANGE PROGRAMS WILL NOT CONTROL THE SPREAD OF AIDS

Part I: Mitchell S. Rosenthal, Part II: Joseph Farah

In Part I of the following two-part viewpoint, Mitchell S. Rosenthal argues that needle exchange programs, which enable injection drug users to replace used needles with sterile ones, have not been proven effective in controlling the spread of HIV infection. Furthermore, he asserts, needle exchange programs will not slow the spread of the AIDS virus through sexual contact between drug users and their partners. In Part II, Joseph Farah contends that needle exchange programs tacitly condone drug use. Funds spent on needle exchange programs would be better used for research on finding a cure for AIDS, he maintains. Rosenthal is president of Phoenix House, a drug rehabilitation agency, and chairman of the New York State Advisory Council on Substance Abuse. Farah is an author, editor, and executive director of the Western Journalism Center in Sacramento, California.

As you read, consider the following questions:

1. What evidence does Rosenthal present to support his contention that the results of the New Haven needle exchange program are flawed?
2. According to Farah, what are three reasons to oppose needle exchange programs?
3. How are needle exchange programs like Russian roulette, in Farah's opinion?

I

Allowing drug users to exchange dirty needles for new ones seems like an enlightened idea—simple, sensible and compassionate. AIDS is rampant among addicts who inject heroin or cocaine, and they transmit the HIV virus to one another by sharing needles and syringes.

But despite all the happy headlines and editorials, there is no evidence that this approach actually works and will reduce transmission of the virus.

QUESTIONABLE ASSUMPTIONS

Let's look at the widely reported "success" of a model needle-exchange program in New Haven, Connecticut. A preliminary report predicted a 33 percent reduction in new infections among addicts in the program. But this result was projected, not achieved. Using a mathematical model, the report forecast, after seven months, what the program would accomplish in a year.

Mathematical models cannot produce valid results unless all the information they include is accurate. The New Haven model makes several questionable assumptions, and the key issue—how needle-sharing behavior has changed—is not addressed directly.

Instead, the returned needles are tracked and tested. When a participant in the program returns someone else's needles, the conclusion is that those needles were shared. But when an addict returns the same needles he or she was issued, it is assumed that the needles were not used by anyone else.

Even if it were possible to discover by this means which needles were shared, it would not reveal how many intravenous drug users were sharing them. By testing, it is possible to discover how many needles are contaminated with the HIV virus, but not how many intravenous drug users have been exposed. Casting further doubt on the New Haven projection is the apparent failure to consider how the high dropout rate—60 percent—might skew the findings.

But premature optimism has put opponents of needle exchange on the defensive, and revealing the study's flaws isn't likely to reduce the pressure for more such programs. Even if it doesn't work, supporters demand, what's the harm in trying? It isn't enough to argue that needle exchange puts government in the bizarre position of abetting illegal and life-threatening behavior that we have been trying desperately to control.

But we can point out that clean needles, even if they could prevent sharing, wouldn't reduce a spread of the AIDS virus from addicts to people who don't use drugs. In the U.S. today, AIDS is being spread most rapidly by heterosexual contact, primarily through transmission of the virus from intravenous drug users to their sexual partners. Clean needles won't alter irresponsible sexual behavior.

Indeed, clean needles aren't going to alter any of the irresponsible and antisocial ways in which drug abusers threaten society. Only treatment can do this. And although clean-needle programs may provide a route to treatment for some drug users, the overwhelming effect would be to impede their movement into treatment.

To be effective, treatment must make demands of drug abusers that few are willing to accept. The great majority will only enter treatment under pressure—and pressure on addicts directly reflects public attitudes about drugs.

By accommodating drug use, through needle exchange, we foster ambivalence, making it harder for communities to discourage drug use and demand that abusers accept treatment.

When we consider this cost and the absence of any proven benefits, we might question whether needle exchange is really such a terrific idea.

II

Imagine finding out that a member of your family or a close friend is shooting drugs. What do you do about it? Do you give him a clean needle? Or do you try to get him into a drug treatment program? Of course, any sensible person is going to try to persuade that friend or family member to get off drugs. That would be the right thing to do, the responsible thing to do.

Nevertheless, in announcing the new national AIDS strategy, President Bill Clinton's top advisors said they would unveil in February 1997 a study backing wider use of needle-exchange programs.

THREE REASONS TO OPPOSE NEEDLE EXCHANGES

There are at least three reasons to oppose federal funding of needle-exchange programs:

• Nowhere in the Constitution is the federal government empowered to spend money on such notions, and Congress has specifically voted to ban such funding.

• This idea is another example of the way some people in our society are, as Senator Daniel Patrick Moynihan (D-N.Y.) would say, defining deviancy down; saying, in effect, that its OK to abuse drugs as long as you use clean needles.

• According to both the politically correct Centers for Disease Control and the National Research Council, there is no empirical evidence to suggest that lives will be saved through needle exchanges. In fact, there is every reason to believe more people will die because of such policies.

So why all the clamor for this new cause du jour? It comes down to the worst kind of political pandering to a tiny special interest group. Sure, everyone can feel better about themselves for allocating taxpayer dollars to needle exchanges, but ultimately it's nothing more than misguided, phony compassion. There is nothing caring about replacing needles. It is another example of symbolism over substance—and worse.

Henry Payne. Reprinted with special permission of United Feature Syndicate.

This idea is the natural extension of the condom distribution scam. The same activist groups promoting needle exchanges continue to insist that condom giveaways are the best way to safeguard people from contracting AIDS sexually. In both cases, however, we are not treating the root problem—namely, irresponsible behavior. In fact, we're condoning it. Just as anal sex, with or without a condom, is risky and potentially deadly, so is drug abuse, with or without clean needles.

How can we justify taking even one dollar away from research into finding a cure for AIDS and spending it on such reckless fantasies? Let's face it. In this age of deficit spending, there is a limited pool of federal money available for all health issues. If some local governments in New York and San Francisco want to experiment with wacky ideas, God bless them. But don't force the rest of us to subsidize their Kevorkian-style madness. [Jack Kevorkian is a Michigan doctor who helps people commit suicide.]

The needle-exchange lunacy is evidence that our society is losing, not only its moral center of gravity, but also its ability to reason—to think logically and respond rationally to political, social and medical problems.

RUSSIAN ROULETTE

Let me give you an analogy: You see a guy playing Russian roulette with two bullets in the chamber. One bullet represents the imminent death a drug user faces from organ failure or accidental overdose, and the other represents the dangers of contracting AIDS. This policy is the legal, moral and practical equivalent of removing one of the bullets and giving the gun back, saying, "OK, continue your game."

Is there any person—let alone society—who wants that on their conscience? Not me.

"Education programs [can] . . . give
participants the skills and self-
confidence to turn from behavior
that would pose a risk to health."

EDUCATION PROGRAMS PREVENT HIGH-RISK BEHAVIOR

James Loyce

James Loyce is the executive director of AIDS Project Los Angeles,
one of the nation's largest AIDS service organizations. In the following viewpoint, Loyce contends that AIDS education programs
can persuade individuals at risk of HIV infection to change their
behavior to reduce their risk. However, he asserts, in order to be
effective, the education programs must be designed for the specific audience they are meant to reach and must help participants
to develop the skills and self-confidence necessary for changing
their behavior.

As you read, consider the following questions:
1. According to Loyce, what should AIDS education programs
   emphasize when working with teenagers?
2. Why are multiple-session education programs better than
   single-session programs, in the author's opinion?
3. How should cost evaluation for education programs be
   measured, according to Loyce?

If I have one piece of advice for parents concerned about sex education for their children on the verge of puberty, it is this: Tell them to resist the urge; tell them to abstain. It is the only—repeat, only—way to be certain that AIDS cannot be transmitted.

Many youngsters—if told carefully, patiently, and frequently about the risks of AIDS and other sexually transmitted diseases by adults they trust—will take that message to heart.

Nevertheless, human nature and hormones being what they are, many others will not heed the message. After all, every adult remembers being young and, with a little exercise of the memory cells, will remember thinking he (or she) would live forever, never get old, and never get sick. For kids who can't be budged from this state of mind, the educational effort must focus on reducing risks.

AIDS is transmitted through bodily fluids, blood and semen. Unlike cold, flu, or tuberculosis viruses, HIV cannot be carried from one person to another by coughing and sneezing. You can't pick it up from using public rest rooms or a knife and fork in a restaurant. It is sexually transmitted, and, before nearly universal screening of the nation's blood supply began nearly 10 years ago, it could be transmitted through transfusions.

AIDS EDUCATION PROGRAMS

AIDS service organizations, such as the one of which I am executive director, AIDS Project Los Angeles, carry out AIDS education programs, working with schools, churches, and other community-centered groups. As is the case with other AIDS service organizations, we only go where we are invited. Our education programs are in business to encourage abstinence and reduce health risks. We do not promote promiscuity; we discourage it.

Over the 14 years in which we have provided support services for people with HIV or full-blown AIDS, our own education programs have evolved to fit the wide variety of audiences we meet in an area of several million people. We have learned that a one-size-fits-all approach to AIDS education does not take into account cultural, age, or social differences.

That did not mean, however, that one community could not usefully apply some AIDS education approaches that had worked elsewhere. With this in mind, our research department set out to find which programs were most effective and efficient. Between May and September 1995, it surveyed more than 700 AIDS risk-reduction sources and reviewed the work of more than 60 community-based AIDS service organizations in 21 states. The programs reviewed spanned a decade, from 1985 to 1995.

If we could successfully identify education programs that were especially successful, our researchers reasoned, information about them could be disseminated and adapted by AIDS service organizations throughout the country.

Unfortunately, the most important finding of our research team is that there is a nearly complete absence of impact-evaluation elements in AIDS risk-reduction education programs. In the 43 cases where our researchers did find that evaluations had been made, most were done on the basis of cost per person reached. That, of course, does not address the question of how many people changed their behavior to avoid or reduce risk as a result of attending AIDS education programs.

Further, there is no national-level standard for measuring the success of these educational efforts. Recently, the Centers for Disease Control has taken a step in the right direction by requiring federally funded AIDS education programs to contain a component for measuring their impact on the behavior of those they serve.

In time, the data developed from these evaluations will give providers of AIDS education programs a means of objectively judging the effectiveness of various approaches. Meanwhile, judgments about what works best must be arrived at on a largely empirical basis. Now that we are 14 years into the AIDS epidemic, the public health professionals organizing these programs are not exactly flying blind. Nevertheless, their decisions about effectiveness are determined mainly by observation and experimentation.

DIFFERENT PROGRAMS FOR DIFFERENT GROUPS

At AIDS Project Los Angeles, for example, this has led to the development of three distinct programs to serve different groups. One, started in 1995, is intended to reach teenagers in general. It is the Student Teacher AIDS Risk Reduction (STARR) program. High school and junior high school students may volunteer to become student teachers. We teach them how to carry the message to their peers. The basic message is that the foundation of any prevention and risk-reduction strategy must be abstinence.

We teach them to make sure their peers understand that 25 percent of all new HIV infections in the United States are in the 24-and-under age-group. We teach them to talk about the primal urge that affects young people; that the urge, mixed with alcohol or drugs, is a powerful combination with unforeseen consequences.

The STARR program is aimed at overcoming the I-am-invincible feeling that young people often have about their bodies. For teenagers who agree to be abstinent, knowledge of how the AIDS virus is transmitted may be sufficient. For others, who do not resist the primal urge, it is essential that an attitude of "I am going to protect myself and my partner" become a basic part of their thinking.

Another of our AIDS education programs is aimed at the group that was most heavily affected during what can be called the "first generation" of the AIDS epidemic: young men who are homosexual or bisexual. In Los Angeles, we organize this program to go to the places where this population congregates.

Education Makes a Difference

A short AIDS-prevention curriculum significantly changed AIDS-related knowledge, beliefs and behaviors among a sample of 867 New York City ninth and 11th graders in 1991. According to an analysis comparing students who took the course with those who did not, the course had a statistically significant positive impact on students' knowledge about AIDS, their beliefs about their susceptibility to infection and about the efficacy of preventive measures, and their participation in risky behaviors. . . . The intervention encouraged favorable change in the likelihood of having sex with high-risk partners, remaining monogamous and using condoms consistently.

L. Remez, *Family Planning Perspectives*, January/February 1994.

Our target audience is the 18-to-25 age-group. One session is organized around a group game modeled after television's *Jeopardy*. It involves risk-reduction educational information and prizes for those who get the right answers. This format helps participants to identify risky behavior and ways to reduce risk. Virtually everyone in this population group knows how the HIV virus is transmitted.

In the eighties, the growth rate of new HIV cases began to decline among homosexual and bisexual men as they modified their behavior to avoid the risks of the disease. Now, however, a new, younger generation has come along that did not experience the suffering and death of friends. Many of its members succumb to the same I-am-invincible feelings that affect their heterosexual contemporaries.

Repetition Is Important

The study our researchers conducted of AIDS education programs around the country made clear that most programs repeat their basic messages over and over again. The messages may be stated in different ways to the same group or to different groups, but repetition is an ingredient widely believed to be necessary if even short-term (one year or less) behavior modification is to be achieved.

Our third program in Los Angeles is tailored to Spanish-speaking young people, both those who speak Spanish more or less exclusively and those who are learning English as a second language at school. We started this program as a sort of "AIDS 101" teaching effort; however, we soon realized that most in our audience had very little idea of the human body and how it works. We restructured the program, after conferring with parent and church groups (this community is closely tied to the Catholic Church).

COMPONENTS THAT REDUCE RISKY BEHAVIOR

Although our survey of AIDS education programs turned up few with data measuring behavior change and actual risk reduction, common threads running through most of them can help us conclude what components are likely to lead to healthy, reduced-risk behavior.

• *Multi-session education programs will tend to show greater short-term behavior changes than will single sessions.* Programs that have a number of sessions can repeat messages and cover a variety of strategies, while time will permit only an overview in a single-session program. A particularly strong presentation in a single session might create a "wake-up" call sufficient to cause six months' worth of behavior change. With a multiple-session program, you might get a year's worth of conscious risk-reduction attitudes on the part of those who participated.

The public health professionals who staff AIDS service organizations see themselves as working against time. The number of reported infections is going up again. Today, heterosexual African American and Hispanic women are among those at greatest risk. Bisexual teenagers are throwing caution to the winds, not realizing that 5 to 10 years from now a dormant virus contracted from reckless behavior may spring to life.

• *Peer-led education can be effective.* If a program participant can identify—by gender and/or cultural background—with the program's leader, he is more likely to gain a heightened appreciation of HIV-related risks. Peer education may include counseling, risk assessment, and service and support referrals. The STARR program for teenagers in Los Angeles uses this approach.

• *Cost evaluation should be measured by the number of infections averted.* James Kahn, of the Institute for Health Policy Studies at the University of California at San Francisco, studied the Santa Barbara (California) Pride Program, which used peer education targeted at young homosexual men and found it to be cost effective. He concluded that it resulted in an 8 percent reduction in sexually risky behavior. He concluded that over five years, approximately 33 cases of HIV infection would be averted in that community because of the program. Using a medical cost estimate of $119,000 per case, he estimated the net savings from this program would be approximately $2.2 million.

• *Knowledge alone is not enough to motivate individuals to avoid risk.* Somewhere between 40,000 and 80,000 new HIV infections occur every year, despite widespread dissemination of information about how the virus is transmitted. While education programs must tirelessly remind those they serve of these facts, they must also give participants the skills and self-confidence to turn from behavior that would pose a risk to health.

A POWERFUL DISEASE

There are some promising drugs under development in the fight against HIV and AIDS, but it is sobering to know that the disease has a gestation period of up to 10 years. Today's careful young adult may have been a carefree teenager a decade ago who became careless and unknowingly infected.

Like most viruses, the HIV virus mutates; it changes more or less continuously. Just as soon as we think science is onto something that will manage the virus and prolong the life of its victims, the virus mutates. Despite the best efforts of some of the nation's finest scientists, HIV and AIDS will be infecting people for a long time.

I am a father with a young daughter. That is why, when she is old enough to be told about these things, I am going to say to her, "Not now. Wait. You will not regret it."

> "Years of AIDS education has probably produced almost no change whatsoever in the behavior that all gay men . . . know to be the most dangerous for transmitting HIV."

EDUCATION PROGRAMS FOR GAY MEN ARE BADLY FLAWED

Walt Odets

Walt Odets asserts in the following viewpoint that AIDS education efforts targeting gay men do not motivate them to adopt safe-sex practices. The education programs often contain misrepresentations about which sexual behaviors increase the risk for contracting HIV and the likelihood of becoming infected, he contends. Therefore, he concludes, many gay men come to believe that they will inevitably contract HIV and do not take measures that would reduce their risk. Odets is a clinical psychologist in Berkeley, California.

As you read, consider the following questions:

1. What is one of the most significant lies perpetuated by AIDS education, in the author's opinion?
2. In the San Francisco City Clinic study cited by the author, how many HIV infections were potentially caused by oral sex?
3. According to Odets, what is the subliminal message gay men receive when they are told to be tested regularly for HIV?

Revised by the author from Walt Odets, "The Fatal Mistakes of AIDS Education," Readings, Harper's Magazine, May 1995, an adaptation of the original article, "AIDS Education and Harm Reduction for Gay Men: Psychological Approaches for the Twenty-first Century," AIDS and Public Policy Journal, vol. 9, no. 1, Spring 1994. Reprinted by permission of the author and University Publishing Group, © 1994.

The AIDS epidemic has now spanned more than a decade, and it seems nearly certain that it will be a lifelong reality for most adult gay men. Gay male communities, especially those in urban centers, have become accustomed to a form of life completely unimaginable ten years ago: a 50 percent overall infection rate, 10 to 40 percent infection rates among segments of the young gay community, and 70 percent rates among older groups. In San Francisco, 30 percent of twenty-year-olds will be infected with or dead of AIDS by age thirty; the majority will become HIV-infected at some point during their lifetime. The mean life expectancy of a San Francisco gay man between the ages of sixteen and twenty-four is currently somewhere around forty-five.

POOR RESULTS

Such figures translate humanly into a huge accumulation of loss and grief. Many gay men are rethinking the purpose and meaning of their lives, and feelings about everything—sexuality, human relations, and death not least of all—have undergone surprising revisions. Yet despite these new realities, public-health approaches to AIDS education have remained largely unchanged since the beginning of the epidemic. As a clinical psychologist with many gay patients, I have observed for several years the poor results and psychological damage our current educational approaches are producing.

Since the early days of the AIDS epidemic, the primary tactic of educators has been to provide people with sensible information and, for those not persuaded by good sense alone, to coerce behavioral change by the power of social compliance. At first, these prevention efforts were assisted by the natural fears that gay men felt. But although education provided the information upon which behavioral changes were built, it is not clear that these efforts ever provided the necessary motivation for change. In this sense, it is not at all clear that our education has ever really "worked."

Despite the concerted efforts of AIDS educators, rates of HIV transmission among gay men began to rise in the mid-Eighties almost as suddenly as they had plummeted only a few years earlier. By 1988 studies of gay men in urban centers were showing that about one third were willing to self-report the practice of unprotected anal intercourse. The real figures are certainly higher and are in fact astonishingly close to the figures we had on anal intercourse before there was an epidemic. In other words, years of AIDS education has probably produced almost no change whatsoever in the behavior that all gay men and their grand-mothers know to be the most dangerous for transmitting HIV.

Unfortunately, a majority of AIDS educators continued to deny "relapse" through several years of soft and hard evidence. They sought to defend the "reputation" of the gay community, asserting that public discussion of the fact of unprotected sex between gay men would jeopardize funding and was therefore "politically naive." They also experienced genuine consternation about what was going on and spent nearly half a decade hoping that relapse was merely an illusion. "I can't believe men are doing this," one San Francisco educator said to me.

A WASTE OF MONEY

Any increased spending on AIDS programs would most likely be misguided. Indeed, a two-year study that we conducted at the University of Chicago indicates that much of the money spent on AIDS has been ineffective in stopping the spread of the epidemic and thus essentially wasted.

AIDS programs have failed, we believe, because government has completely misunderstood the role that human behavior plays in AIDS transmission. As a result, policymakers have devised programs that are as likely to further the spread of AIDS as inhibit it.

Thomas J. Philipson, Richard A. Posner, and John H. Wright, *Perspectives*, Spring 1994.

In early 1992, in the face of overwhelming evidence, AIDS educators finally "went public" with the fact of relapse. Acknowledgment of the problem seemed to be an important start. But the response to relapse since 1992 has revealed a disappointing, often dangerous lack of insight about what men are doing, why they are doing it, and how to address the problem. Educators have largely entrenched themselves still more deeply in earlier approaches, in the belief that they worked at one time and should work again.

MISREPRESENTATIONS

Throughout the epidemic, AIDS education efforts have been marked by misrepresentations—not only withholding information from gay men but lying to them. As with most attempts to mislead people, when the misrepresentations are finally discovered, the useful components of the message will be discarded along with the untruths. Most of the misrepresentations of AIDS education have taken the form of "erring on the safe side," an approach that often makes the entire prevention message seem an impossibility. For many gay men thinking about lifetime forms of sexuality, our message—that every gay man must use a condom every time he participates in any sexual activity—demands an unattainable standard of behavior. The rigidity of that message has contributed to a widely held sense that contracting HIV is inevitable—"not if but when," as one of my patients put it. As a consequence, many gay men engage impulsively or unthinkingly in risky behavior, behavior that really could be avoided, at least most of the time, even over a lifetime. When HIV infection seems inevitable, many men derive comfort from contracting it now, thus eliminating anxiety about when. This is one reason we often see not an increase but a reduction of depression or anxiety in men when they receive positive test results.

One of our most significant and pervasive lies is that "most" gay men are having exclusively protected sex and finding it comfortable, satisfying, and unproblematic. This is not true unless one is speaking strictly of a statistical majority, and even that is in question. Many gay men experience protected sex as restrictive, inadequate, or unacceptable. By hiding this reality behind slogans like "100 percent safe, 100 percent of the time," we force the issue into the closet. There, like closeted homosexuality itself, the practice of unprotected sex develops a secret life with an immense potential for destructiveness. The gay man practicing unprotected sex today is in the closet about it, often without realizing that a majority of his peers are in there with him. Like the closeted homosexual, he experiences shame and guilt, and he begins to form an identity around his feelings and behavior that reinforces rather than inhibits the destructive behavior. Even those who only occasionally practice unprotected sex often feel they have crossed into forbidden territory from which there is no return; many do not even attempt to return. These men are entirely lost to our education.

Oral Sex

The chasm between what we know and what we tell gay men is immense and bewildering. Although there is virtually no significant research from the last decade to support the case for HIV transmission by anything other than receptive anal sex, we continue to force upon gay men unrealistic and exaggerated doubt and anxiety about oral and other forms of sex.

In February 1994, the California AIDS Office released guidelines on oral sex for the first time. What is remarkable and typical of these guidelines is how little research of existing literature went into their formulation, and how marginally the guidelines reflect the research that actually did take place. When I asked California officials about important pieces of research, like a "meta" study of other research by the New York State Department of Health AIDS Institute and an article by Jay Levy in the *American Journal of Medicine*, they seemed never to have heard of them. The New York study reported on one study of 6,704 men in the San Francisco City Clinic Cohort which had found that in five years there were two infections that might be attributed to oral sex. This represents a three one-hundredths of one percent risk of HIV transmission via oral sex over five years. Levy, having conducted a long, detailed discussion of the dangers of anal sex, reported simply that all forms of sex other than anal-receptive intercourse "carry a low but still potential risk of HIV transmission."

Despite the availability of this information, the oral-sex guidelines released to the public not only took an absolutist position on the use of condoms but also insisted that an elaborate regimen of safety precautions be followed. In effect, the guidelines banished to history oral sex as we have known it. It is little wonder that in the weeks following the release of the guidelines, a half-dozen of my psychotherapy patients mentioned the regulations as impossible to adhere to and discouraging generally, and cited them as support for their feelings that the question was not if they would contract HIV but when. One man said to me,

> I know that it's self-destructive, but so far as I'm concerned, it's perfectly natural to want to suck a guy off, and if that's all it takes [to contract HIV], I'm going to get it. I know I'm not going to stop that for the rest of my life. And then I think to myself, "Oh hell, why should I give up all the other things that are important to me [sexually]? I should do what I want, live my life as long as I've got it and get it over with." I can't see trying to hang around for a long life sucking on rubbers. I can't see how other guys do that. Do they do that? I'm asking, because no one I know does. I guess we're all going down the tubes together.

Harmful Instructions

We must carefully examine the almost universal assumption among educators that if we give men "too much information"—which is to say, something like the whole truth to the best of our knowledge—they will abuse it, exercise faulty judgment, or otherwise come up with unintended results. As an educator at the San Francisco AIDS Foundation explained to me, "Directive education is necessary because men need to be told what to do."

The most sacrosanct expression of this approach is the absolute prohibition against saying that when neither partner has HIV, it is acceptable to have anal sex without a condom. As educators, physicians, psychologists, and gay men, we all know or ought to know this is true. Yet the nearly universal response to this assertion by AIDS educators is that such an "admission" would encourage men to do dangerous things. Part of the answer to this objection is obvious. Gay men do not, after all, need AIDS education to be reminded of anal sex; our practice of simply instructing men in behaviors—"a condom every time"— does not allow them to develop the judgment to discern when a particular desired behavior is likely to transmit HIV and when it is not. People thus disempowered by instruction that contradicts their instincts—and often the truth—behave secretly, unthinkingly, and often self-destructively.

HIV TESTS ARE DESTRUCTIVE

Many of the specific educational recommendations that we routinely make to gay men reinforce this fatalistic attitude. The idea that HIV-negative men should test for HIV antibodies every six or twelve months is one such destructive practice. To the extent that it is made explicit at all, the rationale for regular testing is that a man will behave "more responsibly" if he knows he is positive and can seek useful, "early intervention." The truth supports little, if any, of this rationale. We advise men to "play safe" regardless of their HIV status, and researchers have consistently found little behavioral change as a consequence of HIV test results. With existing treatments, medical intervention is generally useless until three to seven years after infection. And knowledge of positive status many years before the onset of clinical illness has been immensely destructive, psychologically, to many gay men.

What recommendations for routine testing do accomplish is to keep the HIV-negative man entangled in irrational fears of infection. By implication, he is being told that he should continue to be tested regularly because regardless of his behavior, he might have contracted HIV. The blanket insistence on protected sex—even between HIV-negative men—only exacerbates the feelings of inevitability that routine testing creates. The ability to have ordinary (unprotected) sex with another HIV-negative man is one of the benefits of being negative; when we tell men that the rule is "a condom every time" regardless of circumstances, we deprive HIV-negative men of one of the most immediate and powerful incentives to remain negative. "If neither of us really has HIV, why are we using condoms?" a psychotherapy patient asked me. "Is it because I might really have HIV? Or Steven might?" Many men express such feelings as well as the related feeling that the very act of putting on a condom makes them feel they must have HIV and are trying to protect their partner from it. We have "double-bound" men into such confusions with a remarkable show of bad psychology that says, in effect:

> Get tested and believe your results. (But if your test is negative, don't believe your results: use a condom anyway.) Safe sex affirms your pride in being gay, and loving gay men protect their partners (from what?). But don't trust your "monogamous" partner (gay men lie and cheat). Feel good about sex: It's natural and it's your right. (But get tested again in six months to see if you've finally gotten yourself into trouble.)

Such education is not a prescription for AIDS prevention, it is a prescription for madness. New approaches to education must tell the truth about these issues, must acknowledge that it is sometimes quite "safe" to have ordinary, unprotected sex, and must help men develop a sense of judgment that would allow them to make the best decisions based on their values and their appraisals of acceptable risk.

THE WRONG PRESCRIPTION

AIDS education must re-evaluate its fundamental purposes. We are not addressing the human needs of the gay community by offering or insisting upon biological survival as the exclusive purpose of human life. Lives must be worth living, and the epidemic itself has already made this more complicated.

The public-health experts and media analysts who now direct our educational efforts must begin to understand and include in those efforts the facts of human experience. One educator, explaining why AIDS prevention was necessarily directive, once said to me, "If you want someone to buy a Chevrolet, you don't tell him he might want a Chevrolet." My answer was that for a man living in a lifelong epidemic in which intimacy might become assault and love become death, we had no Chevrolets, we had only contemplation itself: the internal space for each man to think and feel and thus make for himself the best possible decisions that he might. We cannot tell people how to act in the epidemic any more than we can tell them how to feel about it. It has not worked and will not in the future, and if we are concerned with the quality of gay life in America, rather than merely the quantity, that sort of instruction is something we should not even be trying.

> "Prevention and treatment both require an approach tailored to the particular needs of those afflicted."

EDUCATION PROGRAMS SHOULD TARGET HIGH-RISK GROUPS

John Gagnon

John Gagnon is a professor of sociology at the State University of New York at Stony Brook. In the following viewpoint, Gagnon argues that gay men and intravenous drug users have the highest risk of contracting HIV. Therefore, he maintains, prevention programs should concentrate on these two groups and not on those who are at low risk of contracting the virus. Gagnon contends that directing AIDS prevention programs at groups such as young nondrug-using heterosexuals, who are not at high risk of contracting the disease, wastes precious resources.

As you read, consider the following questions:
1. What is the best hope of fighting AIDS, in Gagnon's opinion?
2. What percentage of Californians with AIDS are gay men, according to the author?
3. According to Gagnon, what are the dangers of a program that recognizes that not all people have an equal risk of contracting HIV?

N ews reports suggest that we are entering a new phase of the AIDS epidemic in which the effectiveness of our prevention efforts will determine how successful we are in fighting the disease. It is a phase for which we are nearly as ill-prepared as we were before 1983, when the cause of AIDS was still unknown.

In spite of the vast amount of money spent on biomedical AIDS research since the mid-1980s, a vaccine for the human immunodeficiency virus appears to be as far away as ever. Antiviral drugs like AZT have marginally increased life expectancy for those infected, but there is still no cure on the horizon.

PREVENTION IS THE BEST HOPE

So for now our best hope of fighting AIDS remains prevention. Yet this fundamental barrier against the virus has been steadily weakened since the mid-1980s by resistance from hostile right-wing groups and by the inertia of Government at all levels. In their prevention campaigns, health officials have failed to focus on the two groups at highest risk of infection, the same ones that were afflicted at the beginning: gay men and intravenous drug users, and their lovers, spouses and children. Instead, they spend precious dollars on diffuse campaigns like the one unveiled in January 1994, in which animated condoms send a message of safer sex aimed largely at heterosexual young adults.

Thus the Government's resources are aimed scattershot at the epidemic. This policy results from a misunderstanding of where the epidemic has been and where it is going. In California, where 80 percent of people living with AIDS are gay men, only 10 percent of prevention dollars are spent on gay men. The New York Times reported on Dec. 11, 1993, that there is evidence of a resurgence of high-risk sexual behavior and infection among young gay men in San Francisco. It is this community, at ground zero of the epidemic, that urgently needs an intensive prevention campaign.

The Government has also failed to reach out adequately to the men and women who are in danger of infection through intravenous drug use—the same people who are found in jails and prisons, among the homeless and those without either drug treatment services or clean needles.

We need to recognize that the AIDS epidemic is actually a number of micro-epidemics. Prevention and treatment both require an approach tailored to the particular needs of those afflicted.

THE GREATER DANGER

What are the dangers of implementing a policy based on the recognition that not everyone is equally at risk? Some argue that if those in the mainstream believe that the epidemic is unlikely to affect them they will abandon those at the margins of society who remain at the highest risk. A far greater danger, however, is the rising rate of infection in high-risk communities because inadequate prevention resources are too thinly spread.

It is not that all Americans shouldn't be informed about the risks of infection; there will inevitably be some transmissions of the H.I.V. virus among groups at relatively low risk. The advice that is given low-risk groups about how to avoid H.I.V. infection should be as plain-spoken as the information given to those at high risk.

AN INEFFECTIVE WAY TO FIGHT AIDS

Propagandizing the whole nation about condom use is a stupefyingly ineffective way to fight AIDS. Hunters rarely succeed by spraying shotgun pellets randomly in all directions all day. It's usually better to aim directly at the duck. In this case, the ducks are the relatively small high-risk populations who engage in anal sex or intravenous drug use.

John Leo, *Washington Times*, January 12, 1994.

I live in New York City. I am in little danger of my house burning down in a wildfire or being swept away in a flood, but I happily support Government efforts to prevent these disasters or help those who have been in harm's way. I have not argued that these people knew the risks of fire or flood when they decided to live in Malibu or Omaha, and that therefore they do not deserve a national response.

We now have a President [Bill Clinton] who appears to acknowledge that AIDS is a national disaster. Perhaps he will respond to the epidemic in a way that truly recognizes who is ill and who is at risk and treats them like all Americans who have been in harm's way.

PERIODICAL BIBLIOGRAPHY

The following articles have been selected to supplement the diverse views presented in this chapter. Addresses are provided for periodicals not indexed in the *Readers' Guide to Periodical Literature*, the *Alternative Press Index*, the *Social Sciences Index*, or the *Index to Legal Periodicals and Books*.

Stephen Arrendell	"Panic in Needle Park," POZ, November 1996. Available from 349 W. Twelfth St., New York, NY 10014-1721.
Rick Bluthenthal	"Combating the AIDS Pandemic," *Crossroads*, November 1995.
I. MacAllister Booth	"Ending the AIDS Pandemic," *Vital Speeches of the Day*, March 15, 1994.
Midge Decter	"Homosexuality and the Schools," *Commentary*, March 1993.
Glamour	"A New Safe-Sex Method for Women Needs Your Attention," May 1994.
Christine Gorman	"The Exorcists," *Time*, Fall 1996.
Issues and Controversies On File	"Needle-Exchange Programs," October 25, 1996. Available from Facts On File, 11 Penn Plaza, New York, NY 10001-2006.
Alexia Lewnes	"Streetwise," *City Limits*, August/September 1995.
Douglas Martin	"Dispensing Needles, Not Judgment," *New York Times*, November 7, 1996.
Cindy Patton	"Global Warning," POZ, August/September 1996.
Mark Schoofs	"The Great Fellatio Debate: How Safe Is Oral Sex?" *Village Voice*, October 15, 1996. Available from 36 Cooper Sq., New York, NY 10003.
Elizabeth Taylor	"You Can Never Say Enough," *Omni*, January 1995.
Germaine O'Malley Wensley	"Condoms in the School: A Case of Educational Malpractice," *Family*, March 1993. Available from 50 St. Paul's Ave., Boston, MA 02130.

CHAPTER 4

HOW CAN AIDS BE TREATED?

CHAPTER PREFACE

In November 1996, Arizona and California voters approved propositions that legalized the medical use of marijuana. According to proponents of these propositions, medicinal marijuana can effectively relieve some symptoms of AIDS, cancer, and other illnesses.

Indeed, many researchers and physicians maintain that marijuana alleviates the nausea, vomiting, and loss of appetite caused by AIDS and highly toxic drugs such as AZT. According to San Francisco writers Stephen LeBlanc and Jeff Getty, "Marijuana is medically necessary and beneficial for people with AIDS with wasting and nausea." Furthermore, advocates of medicinal marijuana cite studies by the National Institute on Drug Abuse, Harvard University, and other groups describing the medical benefits of the drug.

But other observers contend that marijuana has little or no medical value and warn that its use can cause harmful side effects. In the words of New York University professor of medicine Gabriel Nahas, "There is no medical justification for the use of marijuana smoking in the treatment of nausea and vomiting associated with cancer or AIDS chemotherapy." Nahas and other experts assert that prolonged marijuana smoking causes a variety of health problems, including emphysema-like symptoms, various cancers, impairment of memory and psychomotor performance, psychological dependence, and lethargy.

Although several state legislatures have considered bills similar to the Arizona and California propositions, the federal government continues to classify the drug as an illegal substance with no medical application. The medicinal use of marijuana is one of the issues debated in the following chapter on how AIDS can be treated.

| "It is reasonable to imagine that virus production will be effectively shut down."

DRUG COMBINATIONS CAN INHIBIT THE AIDS VIRUS

Jerome Groopman

Researchers have reported that a combination of drugs can greatly reduce the amount of HIV in the human bloodstream—sometimes to undetectable levels. In the following viewpoint, Jerome Groopman argues that a combination of AZT, 3TC, and a protease inhibitor can both reduce HIV levels and bolster the human immune system. Groopman is a professor of medicine at Harvard University Medical School and the director of the Mapplethorpe Laboratory for AIDS Research at Beth-Israel Deaconess Hospital, both in Boston.

As you read, consider the following questions:

1. How has HIV reacted to treatments applied against it, according to Groopman?
2. According to Groopman, what are "sanctuary sites"?
3. How are computers being used to help inhibit the integrase enzyme, according to the author?

From Jerome Groopman, "Chasing the Cure," New Republic, August 12, 1996. Reprinted by permission of The New Republic, ©1996, The New Republic, Inc.

The AIDS Conference held in July 1996 in Vancouver celebrated a turning point in the battle against the human immune deficiency virus (HIV). For the first time, a true clinical remission of the disease was reported. Talk of a cure for the great health scourge of our time filled the halls.

In 1995, AIDS researchers, myself included, expressed cautious optimism in the fight against AIDS. The hope was that a combination of drugs such as AZT and 3TC, which slow the rate at which the virus replicates, and protease inhibitors, which drastically reduce the amount of virus in the body, could improve the health of AIDS patients. It has. With this triple combination—AZT, 3TC and a protease inhibitor—virus production slowed ten- to 100-fold, and the capacity of the immune system to defend itself from viral attack grew. It now appears this treatment could add many years of productive life.

But do these inroads against AIDS amount to a cure? It's too early to say yes. There's not yet enough evidence to conclude that this combination completely inhibits HIV, or that its effects can be sustained indefinitely.

HIV's Destructiveness

For one thing, the virus is remarkably resilient. It mutates and grows resistant to the treatments applied against it. The virus also reproduces in certain areas of the body, such as the brain, lymph nodes and testes (called "sanctuary sites"), where current antiviral drugs still don't penetrate well. For many of the treated patients, the drug therapy bolstered their immune systems markedly, yet still didn't return them to full strength. This less-than-complete recovery suggests that, for these patients, HIV may still be at work in their sanctuary sites, where it is actively killing T-cells, which guard against deadly infections.

But that doesn't mean a cure is unattainable. Based on the success and limitations of triple drug therapy, three strategic aims emerge. First, to develop enough novel and complementary therapies to paralyze the virus completely and prevent it from mutating anew or otherwise becoming resistant to further drug treatment. Next, to deliver these effective drug combinations to the hard-to-reach sanctuary sites. Finally, to restore each patient's immune defenses. All three objectives can probably be achieved.

The human immune deficiency virus is a parasite; it cannot exist or reproduce outside certain blood cells—the now-famous T-4 cells and macrophages of the immune system. But the damage it does—although limited to a tiny proportion of blood cells—is devastating. It not only blocks the normal defense functions of the immune system's T-cells, it remakes them into breeders of a new virus and ultimately drains them of life. As T-cells and macrophages are destroyed, the body's defenses against infection and cancer are lost.

STEPS TO UNDERSTANDING AND STOPPING HIV

Key to continuing the fight to prevent AIDS is understanding the precise and discrete steps in the virus's disabling of the immune system cells. It allows us to create a variety of therapies to prevent or even disengage the virus's fatal embrace of the cell. Each step needs its own description.

HOW PROTEASE INHIBITORS WORK

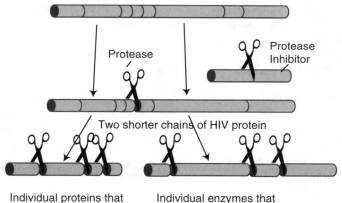

Protease

Protease Inhibitor

Two shorter chains of HIV protein

Individual proteins that make new HIV particles

Individual enzymes that help build new HIV particles

Protease inhibitors prevent HIV's protease enzyme from cutting long strands of proteins and enzymes into the shorter pieces that the virus needs in order to replicate.

Source: Adapted from The Body, www.thebody.com.

Step One: Infection. Obviously, it's to our advantage to stop HIV before it infects new cells. To do this, we have to know how HIV spreads. And we've come to understand that process better. When HIV encounters its prey, it grabs hold of the T-cell or macrophage by two distinct handles. The first, which has been known to researchers for a decade, is called CD4. The second is termed a serpentine chemokine receptor because it snakes through the surface of the cell. This second serpentine handle was identified only in 1996, and its discovery marks an important advance. It provides the key to creating new drugs designed to block HIV from attaching to uninfected cells—stopping its advance cold.

Step Two: Blueprinting. Next, after HIV penetrates the cell, the virus copies its genetic blueprint from an RNA form into DNA. A viral enzyme called reverse transcriptase is central to this process. The goal here is to reduce the ability of the virus to copy its blueprint. This limits the virus from imposing its genetic program on the cell's.

So far, the main treatments at this stage have been the drugs AZT and 3TC, which poison reverse transcriptase, the critical enzyme. And so far these drugs have been moderately successful in slowing the replication process. But now Boehringer Ingelheim has developed a different kind of drug called nevirapine. Like AZT and 3TC, nevirapine also poisons the reverse transcriptase, though in a different fashion. Studies presented in Vancouver indicate that mixing these two types of poisons greatly enhances their potency against HIV, without harming the host. By inhibiting the pernicious enzyme at multiple sites, the combination makes it harder for the virus to grow resistant.

IN THE NUCLEUS

Step Three: Integration. If the DNA blueprint is successfully copied, the virus inserts itself into the nucleus of the cell. At this critical step, the virus takes hold of the cell's command center. Again, there's a key viral enzyme at work, one called integrase, which integrates the viral genes into those of the host.

Treatments at this stage of the infection have been slow to come. But computers are helping to map the three-dimensional structure of the integrase enzyme. Then, using the topology of the enzyme, the computers can design specific chemicals to inhibit the integrase. This approach succeeded in creating the protease inhibitors, and there's promise it will succeed here as well.

Step Four: Exportation. At the fourth stage of infection, a viral protein called Rev helps carry the instructions of the integrated blueprint from the nucleus out into the cytoplasm, or body, of the cell. There new viruses are constructed. Our laboratory and others have created "blockers" that in test-tube experiments prevent Rev from grabbing hold of and then transporting the blueprints. If the blueprints are locked in the center of the cell, they are useless in providing the needed design for production of HIV.

SIGNS OF PROGRESS

Step Five: New Viruses. The final steps in the life cycle of HIV involve assembling new viruses that exit the cell and then attack new prey. It is here that the powerful protease inhibitors work, disrupting the assembly. So far, these protease inhibitors—which are, after all, still relatively new—have their limits. They must be taken several times a day; they produce side effects of nausea, diarrhea and kidney stones; and, most important, they haven't deeply penetrated sanctuary sites. But the second generation of these drugs, some of which are already in clinical trials, show signs of working better.

Although HIV will try to elude these therapies, mutating and changing form to detour around the roadblocks placed in its path, there are limits to the contortions it can undergo. How many high hurdles are needed to stop the virus definitively? No one knows. We learned in Vancouver, however, that three drugs in combination cause the microbe to stumble severely. As we improve drug delivery to sanctuary sites, as we add both agents such as nevirapine and blockers of attachment, of integrase and of Rev, it is reasonable to imagine that virus production will be effectively shut down. Uncoupled from the virus's fatal embrace, the immune system may well be able to regenerate, like a bulb that returns in full blossom after a long winter. We still do not have a cure, but the question has become "when" rather than "if."

"For every person who succeeds on the [drug combination] therapies, there seems to be another who has found them . . . unwieldy, toxic and ineffective."

DRUG COMBINATIONS MAY NOT INHIBIT THE AIDS VIRUS

Jeffrey L. Reynolds

In the following viewpoint, Jeffrey L. Reynolds argues that drug combinations being promoted as a successful treatment for AIDS actually do not reduce HIV levels in many AIDS patients and even make some patients much sicker. Furthermore, he maintains, because of the drugs' high cost and complicated regimen, a great number of AIDS patients—notably the poor—will not be able to take them. Reynolds contends that inconsistent use of these drugs, which often occurs because of their high cost and difficult regimen, may help HIV build resistance to them. Reynolds is the director of public policy and public relations for the Long Island Association for AIDS Care in Huntington Station, New York.

As you read, consider the following questions:
1. According to Jeanne Carey, cited by Reynolds, what are the side effects of protease inhibitors?
2. In the author's opinion, what groups of people are AIDS prevention efforts failing to reach?
3. What is Directly Observed Therapy, according to Reynolds?

From Jeffrey L. Reynolds, "Listening to Protease," In These Times, February 3, 1997. Reprinted by permission of In These Times.

For Sara Klymer, as for many people living with AIDS, 1996 seemed to mark a turning point. After five years of battling HIV with an endless array of ineffective and often toxic drugs, the 34-year-old Long Island mother of two says she'll never forget the euphoria she felt as she read about the treatment revolution unfolding at 1996's Ninth International Conference on AIDS. "I had no idea what a protease inhibitor was, but it sure sounded like the cure I never imagined I'd live to see," she said, referring to the much-ballyhooed class of powerful drugs.

Unlike earlier drugs, protease inhibitors limit HIV's ability to reproduce. Less virus in a person's body means less damage to his or her immune system and, generally, better health. Although scientists now speak in confusing terms about using the drugs to "eradicate" HIV and to reduce the virus to levels that are undetectable using current technologies, complete elimination of HIV remains the unattained holy grail of AIDS research. Still, taken together with fresh insights about how HIV attacks the immune system and better lab tests for predicting the progression of the disease, protease inhibitors seem to hold the long-awaited promise of transforming a fatal illness into a manageable chronic condition—an important step on the way to a cure.

FROM HOPE TO DISAPPOINTMENT

Sara likened the breakthroughs to a death-row pardon. By early August 1996, she was on a drug cocktail that included saquinivir, the first protease inhibitor to gain approval from the Food and Drug Administration, as well as two older antivirals, AZT and 3TC. Though she describes the regimen as grueling and the side effects as "just this side of death," she says the prospect of returning to work, watching her kids get married, and living rather than dying made it all worth it.

But this carefully chosen trade-off began to fall apart in October 1996, when a much-anticipated blood test showed that the drugs were having little effect on the levels of the virus. Her doctor quickly dismissed the disappointing results as an aberration and swapped the saquinivir for indinivir, also known as Crixivan, the most popular protease inhibitor, taken by an estimated 60,000 Americans as of 1997. By the end of the year, Sara had lost 15 pounds, and her viral levels remained virtually unchanged. "I started to wonder what was wrong with me or what I had done wrong and kept praying that eventually the drugs would kick in," she says. They never did. She started 1997 with a new game plan that includes plenty of vitamins, herbs and acupuncture, but no protease inhibitors.

AIDS sufferers' mad dash for the drugs is understandable, given the endless stream of prominently placed features in the mainstream press that have recounted tales of patients miraculously pulled from their deathbeds by the arsenal of potent medications. A *Newsweek* cover story in November 1996 mused about "the end of AIDS," while noted author, editor and AIDS survivor Andrew Sullivan penned an 8,000-word tome for the *New York Times Magazine* about the "twilight" of the epidemic—not as a prospect for the future, but as a present-day reality.

PROMISE FOR SOME, NOT FOR OTHERS

Given the current atmosphere of celebration and the genuine success some have experienced with the drugs, Sara's story seems like a shocking anomaly, but it's not. For every person who succeeds on the therapies, there seems to be another who has found them to be just as unwieldy, toxic and ineffective as the '80s AIDS wonder drug AZT. The three protease inhibitors now available to the general public were approved and rushed to the market in record time based on a small number of short-term clinical trials involving just a few drug combinations and enrollees that met specific criteria. Why the rush? Because people are dying. Why the hype? Because after years of never-ending losses and snail-paced progress, protease inhibitors seem to represent a new dawn on the AIDS front, and hope, however precarious, has been renewed.

After years of yelling, screaming and demanding access to better treatments, AIDS activists seem to have got what they were asking for. But treatment, however unproven, is not synonymous with access—especially in a global context.While the drugs hold promise for some, the great majority of the world's 22 million men, women and children with AIDS will die before ever hearing the words protease inhibitor, much less being able to afford the $15,000 to $20,000 annual price tag.

OBSTACLES TO TREATMENT

These economic and social disparities make even the most promising medical developments meaningless not only in Third World countries, but also in the growing number of Third World–like communities in the United States. Only those with the right body chemistry, a stroke of luck and the economic, social and emotional resources necessary to follow the complicated regimen will get a shot at renewed health, stamina and a new lease on life.

"I'd dare anyone to maintain the schedule and regimen," says

Brendan Pierce, a physician's assistant at the SUNY [State University of New York] Health Sciences Center in Brooklyn. Life on protease inhibitors means taking up to 30 pills a day at the correct times, in the correct order and with the correct foods. Some must be taken on an empty stomach, others without fatty foods—a difficult task for those who depend on handouts and soup kitchens for their meals. Aside from the need for consistency, there are few gold standards in terms of when to start therapy and which combinations to use. A survey of AIDS doctors conducted by Gay Men's Health Crisis in New York found that almost no two doctors were using the drugs alike or counseling patients in the same way.

DRAWBACKS OF THE DRUGS

Because even a small number of missed or inconsistent dosages can give HIV the window of opportunity it needs to build resistance and render the drugs useless, Pierce says he won't prescribe protease inhibitors to those he deems likely to stumble on the regimen—about 70 percent of his patients. "If I have a drug user who I know is not being compliant, I won't prescribe a protease inhibitor at that point; instead I'll aggressively treat opportunistic infections and prescribe nutritional supplements," he explains. "Coupling drug use with a protease-inhibitor regimen is a disaster, especially coupled with the current environment of criminalization and the lack of reasonable support for the active user."

For many people infected with HIV, compliance is further diminished by a host of side effects—reportedly more severe in women—that make life on the drugs unbearable. "Some prescribing is being done by practitioners who fail to counsel patients about the risks of nonadherence or what they can reasonably expect from the medications," says Dr. Jeanne Carey, a physician at Beth Israel Hospital's HIV Comprehensive Care Center in Manhattan. Contrary to the drug manufacturers' claims of high tolerance, Carey estimates that 70 percent of those on protease inhibitors suffer nausea and diarrhea every day. "It's a complicated thing," she explains, "to talk to a person about how much they're willing to change their lives in order to take these medications, and to tell them that if you take the medications as prescribed, the numbers on your lab sheets will look better, but that's not quality of life."

Chris Jackson couldn't agree more. Diagnosed with HIV in 1987 and relatively symptom-free and healthy since that time, the Long Island 38-year-old decided to try Crixivan for six months. She describes her adherence to the arduous regimen as "meticulous," and within three months her HIV levels dropped from a fairly high 200,000 viruses per milliliter of plasma to undetectable levels. A stunning success, in other words? Not according to Chris, who is also diabetic. "My blood sugars were uncontrollable, my kidneys hurt, I couldn't sleep, and when I walked up a flight of stairs, I had to sit down for 15 minutes," she says. "The rest of your body is falling apart, but you're not dying of AIDS." Chris says her doctor pressured her to stay on Crixivan, but she refused, went off the drug and has never felt better.

SETTING BACK AIDS PREVENTION

The lionized medical advances in the fight against AIDS can also work at cross-purposes with public-health policies designed to slow the spread of the virus. Prevention efforts to date have failed to adequately reach many people of color, drug users, teens and women, all groups among whom infection rates continue to climb. Now the growing notion that AIDS is no longer fatal reduces the perceived danger of a disease that already seems like a comfortably distant threat to most people. Unsafe injection practices are once again becoming common. And buoyed by speculation that lower viral levels in a person's body may reduce the possibility of infecting others, many gay men—especially younger men—are returning to unsafe sex.

OPPORTUNITY FOR DRUG RESISTANCE REMAINS

Even with the most powerful of the antiretroviral combination approaches, some degree of viral replication will still occur. As long as there is any viral replication occurring at all, the opportunity for the creation of new virus that is resistant to the effects of a given drug (or drugs) remains. The possibility of the emergence of drug-resistant HIV mutants will only cease to be a problem when all the virus in the body has been eradicated.

Mike Barr, *Community Prescription Service InfoPack*, Fall 1996.

The last decade's tenuous progress in AIDS prevention may be further set back by the spread of protease-inhibitor-resistant strains of HIV. Within a month of starting a combination of AZT, 3TC and saquinivir in May 1996, Greg Fauth knew something wasn't right. "I felt like someone beat the hell out of me, like I was going to die, and so much worse than ever before," laments the 41-year-old recovering drug addict who, against his doctor's advice, now takes the drugs sporadically. Fauth gives the leftover medication away to his friends without health insurance, Medicaid or other means of financing the expensive drugs, many of whom also only take the drugs sporadically.

Studies suggest that between 10 percent to 20 percent of those newly diagnosed as HIV-positive have been infected with a strain of the virus that is resistant to AZT from the start. So the emergence of a much stronger variety of HIV within the next few years is a significant threat. Irregular use of protease inhibitors encourages the development of protease-resistant strains. It's precisely this potential that has prompted officials like San Francisco Public Health Director Sandra Hernandez to wonder aloud about Directly Observed Therapy, in which doctors monitor AIDS patients to be sure they are taking the medication on schedule. Drawing a parallel to efforts to control multi-drug-resistant tuberculosis (TB), Hernandez in 1996 suggested making protease-inhibitor therapy mandatory and having the health department supervise a schedule of dosages for the noncompliant. There is, however, a world of difference between the two diseases. Not only is tuberculosis transmitted far more easily than HIV, but TB medications completely cure the disease within a few months, are only taken once a day, and don't have serious side effects. Hernandez quickly retracted her comments in the face of a fiery response from AIDS activists.

SOCIAL ISSUES

AIDS funding battles have always been the epidemic's most contentious. The alluring potential of protease inhibitors has reignited nasty disagreements about how federal Ryan White CARE [Comprehensive AIDS Resources Emergency] Act dollars should be divided. An article in the *Wall Street Journal* quoted AIDS Memorial Quilt founder Cleve Jones and other prominent activists as saying that drugs, treatment and research should replace social and community-based services as the AIDS funding priority. Michael T. Isbell, associate executive director of Gay Men's Health Crisis, agrees that "access to the new drugs should be the number-one priority," but also believes that consumers are going to require services that make access to care meaningful. "We are seeing people with multiple psychosocial issues," says Isbell, "and if you don't have a roof over your head, or food to eat, you don't stand a good chance of maintaining the therapies."

If nothing else, protease inhibitors are further proof of the undeniable link between our individual and collective immune systems. Doing battle with HIV means confronting not only a relentless virus, but the persistent social epidemics of poverty, homelessness and substance abuse that plague the disadvantaged populations that make up the majority of new cases.

Whether we've truly turned a corner in the AIDS crisis remains to be seen. That will be determined largely by our ability to improve the tolerability and efficacy of protease inhibitors, to enhance access to those without, and to stick with public education efforts. Most importantly, protease inhibitors remind us that the fight against AIDS won't be won in the laboratory, but in our communities, where we must strengthen our response to a virus that thrives on complacency.

| "There is strong scientific evidence that marijuana is a safe and effective medicine."

MEDICAL MARIJUANA SHOULD BE LEGALIZED FOR USE BY AIDS PATIENTS

Kevin B. Zeese

In 1996, Arizona and California voters approved propositions that legalized the medical use of marijuana. In the following viewpoint, Kevin B. Zeese asserts that medical marijuana can improve the health of patients with AIDS, cancer, and other illnesses. Zeese contends that marijuana can increase AIDS patients' appetites and relieve their nausea and vomiting. Lower dosage levels and easier ingestion make smoked marijuana a more ideal medicine than a legalized pill that contains a synthetic marijuana ingredient, he maintains. Zeese is the president of Common Sense for Drug Policy, a Falls Church, Virginia, organization that seeks to inform the public about drug policy.

As you read, consider the following questions:

1. For how long has marijuana been used medically, according to Zeese?
2. According to the author, what did state studies in Michigan and New Mexico find?
3. In Zeese's opinion, what type of approach should the federal government take toward medical marijuana?

Excerpted from Kevin B. Zeese, "Research Findings on Medicinal Properties of Marijuana," 1997 (cited January 1997); World Wide Web, http://www.lindesmith.org. Reprinted by permission of the author.

With the passage of initiatives in California and Arizona, the debate about the medical utility of marijuana is in the spotlight once again. On December 30, 1996, the federal government announced that it intends to use its authority to stop doctors from recommending or prescribing marijuana to their patients. . . .

In their memorandum, the Clinton Administration described a public relations effort with medical associations and the public reinforcing the message that marijuana has no medical value. On December 29, 1996, retired General Barry McCaffrey, the nation's drug czar, claimed in a column syndicated by the Scripps-Howard News Service that "no clinical evidence demonstrates that smoked marijuana is good medicine."

THE HISTORY OF MEDICAL MARIJUANA

Marijuana has long been recognized as having medical properties. Indeed, its medical use predates recorded history. The earliest written reference is to be found in the fifteenth century B.C., Chinese Pharmacopeia, the Ry-Ya. Between 1840 and 1900, more than 100 articles on the therapeutic use of cannabis were published in medical journals. The federal government in its 1974 report *Marihuana and Health* states:

> The modern phase of therapeutic use of cannabis began about 140 years ago when W.B. O'Shaughnessy reported on its effectiveness as an analgesic and anticonvulsant. At about the same time K. Moreau de Tours described its use in melancholia and other psychiatric illnesses. Those who saw favorable results observed that cannabis produced sleep, enhanced appetite and did not cause physical addiction.

The 1975 report of the federal government began its discussion of medical marijuana by stating, "Cannabis is one of the most ancient healing drugs." The report further noted: "One should not, however, summarily dismiss the possibility of therapeutic usefulness simply because the plant is the subject of current sociopolitical controversy.". . .

MODERN RESEARCH FINDINGS

There has been a tidal wave of published research demonstrating marijuana's medical usefulness. Indeed, it is stated in the research studies conducted by various states under FDA [Food and Drug Administration] protocol that the research being conducted was in the final phase of approval by the FDA. When the federal government stopped research on the medical use of marijuana in 1992, the drug had nearly completed the requirements for new drug approval.

Drug Czar Barry McCaffrey's assertion in his Scripps-Howard News Service column that "no clinical evidence demonstrates that smoked marijuana is good medicine" is inconsistent with the facts. Whether this is an intentional deception, as part of the federal government's stated public relations offensive against medical marijuana, or whether it is based on ignorance does not matter. The reality is General McCaffrey's statements are not consistent with the facts. . . .

Doctors have a sound basis on which to recommend marijuana for use by their patients. Indeed, physicians are well aware of the medical value of marijuana. One study, a scientific survey of oncologists, found that almost one-half (48 percent) of the cancer specialists responding would prescribe marijuana to some of their patients if it were legal. In fact, over 44 percent reported having recommended the illegal use of marijuana for the control of nausea and vomiting. . . .

THERAPY FOR AIDS PATIENTS

Cancer research is relevant to marijuana as a useful therapy for AIDS patients. The same symptoms need to be controlled among AIDS patients: appetite, nausea and vomiting. There have been recent reports of AIDS and marijuana in the literature. A study with THC [tetrahydrocannabinol, the main active ingredient in marijuana] found relief of nausea and significant weight gain in 70 percent of patients. However, one-fifth of the patients did not like the psychoactive effects of synthetic THC, indicating marijuana is likely to be preferred by AIDS patients. This is consistent with a survey of people with AIDS conducted by a researcher in Hawaii in 1996. The survey found that 98.4 percent of AIDS patients were aware of the medical value of marijuana and 36.9 percent had used it as an antiemetic. Of those that had used it, 80 percent preferred it over prescription drugs including synthetic THC. A study conducted in Australia of HIV patients found that those who used marijuana had a better quality of life. In particular, those that were HIV positive for over ten years found marijuana to be critical. One patient told the researcher that he considered marijuana to be his savior. . . .

In addition to the published research there have been a series of six studies conducted by state health departments under research protocols approved by the U.S. Food and Drug Administration. The focus of these studies, conducted by six state health agencies, was the use of marijuana as an antiemetic for cancer patients. The studies, conducted in California, Georgia, New Mexico, New York, Michigan and Tennessee, compared marijuana to antiemetics available by prescription, including the synthetic THC pill, Marinol. Marijuana was found to be an effective and safe antiemetic in each of the studies and more effective than other drugs for many patients. . . .

STUDIES OF MARIJUANA CONSTITUENTS

In addition to research on smoked marijuana there has been a host of research on constituents of marijuana. This research is relevant in measuring the effectiveness of marijuana.

The drug for which there has been the most research is the THC pill. This pill contains pure delta-9-tetrahydrocannabinol in sesame seed oil. This substance is now scheduled in Schedule II of the Controlled Substances Act. When the drug was rescheduled, the Food and Drug Administration acknowledged: "The effects of pure THC are essentially similar to those of cannabis containing THC in equivalent amounts." Thus, the federal government has acknowledged that THC, which is available as a medicine, adequately emulates the effectiveness of marijuana. In fact, the [state health studies] show that marijuana is in fact a more effective medicine than the THC pill.

The research which compares marijuana to the THC pill found that patients preferred marijuana to THC and that marijuana was more effective at treating symptoms. State studies in Michigan and New Mexico found that most patients who tried THC chose to use marijuana instead. The most common reasons for this choice were because THC was more psychoactive, erratic and unpredictable. Patients found they had more control and a quicker response with smoked marijuana than with oral THC. Patients found it difficult to swallow the pill when they were nauseous. Patients were also able to limit their use of marijuana to only the amount needed when it was smoked. For many cancer and AIDS patients this can involve smoking a very small quantity of the drug. With the THC pill the patient must ingest the whole pill and therefore cannot control the dose. . . .

RESOLVING THE MEDICAL MARIJUANA PROBLEM

There is strong scientific evidence that marijuana is a safe and effective medicine. The voters in California and Arizona have recognized this at the ballot box. It is time for the federal government to help resolve this problem rather than threaten doctors with sanctions for providing medical advice to their patients and denying seriously ill patients access to a much-needed medicine.

The California and Arizona initiatives, as well as state laws in two dozen states, provide an opportunity to resolve the medical marijuana problem. Research on the safety and effectiveness of marijuana is in its final phase. All that is needed is late-Phase III research. These are broad-based research studies which result in large numbers of patients receiving marijuana.

The federal government, in its policy announcement of December 30, 1996, stated that it wanted to ensure the integrity of the drug approval process. Part of their plan to do so includes reviewing the research and seeking to fill gaps in research with new research.

| MARIJUANA RELIEF

Marijuana alleviates the nausea, vomiting, and the loss of appetite caused by the AIDS wasting syndrome and by treatment with AZT and other drugs without accelerating the rate at which HIV positive individuals develop clinical AIDS or other illnesses.

Paul Armentano, *Freedom@NORML*, November 1996.

Combining the Food and Drug Administration's need for late-Phase III research before they approve marijuana as a medicine with the decision of voters in California and Arizona to make marijuana medically available will satisfy two needs. It can make marijuana available to large numbers of people under a research umbrella. (In the early 1980s nearly 1,000 patients a year were using marijuana medically under federally approved research programs. In fact, one year California requested one million medical marijuana cigarettes from the FDA.) In addition, it could finally resolve the medical marijuana problem and make marijuana available as a medicine by prescription.

GETTING RESULTS

The Food and Drug Administration should contact the health departments of Arizona, California and other states which have expressed interest in medical marijuana and ask them to participate in the final Phase III studies needed to complete the new drug application process. Getting results from this research should take less than one year. If they are consistent with previous research it should result in marijuana becoming a prescription drug under Schedule II of the Controlled Substances Act. Such a process will restore the integrity of the medical scientific process of drug approval which has been undermined by the use of medical marijuana as a political tool by those favoring expanded drug war policies.

By taking a constructive approach, rather than a confrontational one, the federal government avoids conflict with state law, does not intrude on the doctor-patient relationship and ensures that, in the end, marijuana is only made available as a prescription medicine to the seriously ill. Arizona and California have presented an opportunity to resolve an issue that is long overdue for resolution.

| "No clinical evidence demonstrates that smoked marijuana is good medicine."

MEDICAL MARIJUANA SHOULD NOT BE LEGALIZED FOR USE BY AIDS PATIENTS

Barry R. McCaffrey

Barry R. McCaffrey is America's "drug czar," or director of the federal Office of National Drug Control Policy. In the following viewpoint, McCaffrey argues that the passage in 1996 of Arizona and California initiatives legalizing the medical use of marijuana sends the wrong message to Americans, particularly youths. There is no clinical evidence to support the use of smoked marijuana as a medicine for AIDS and other diseases, McCaffrey contends. Smoked marijuana is a dangerous drug, he asserts, that can harm the immune systems of AIDS patients. McCaffrey insists that legal medications—such as pills that contain the synthetic form of marijuana's active ingredient—are safer and more effective than smoked marijuana.

As you read, consider the following questions:
1. In McCaffrey's opinion, what factor helped the Arizona and California propositions to win?
2. How is smoked marijuana more harmful than other oral medications, according to McCaffrey?
3. According to the author, what is the function of the Controlled Substances Act?

Excerpted from Barry R. McCaffrey, statement to the Senate Committee on the Judiciary, December 2, 1996.

Having worked with the Congress and members of this [Senate judiciary] committee for nine months to reduce drug use and its consequences in America, I share your concern that these two measures [Arizona and California propositions legalizing the medical use of marijuana] threaten to undermine our efforts to protect our children from dangerous psychoactive drugs. It would not be an exaggeration to say that the very essence of our National Drug Control Strategy—our resolve to prevent the 68 million Americans under the age of 18 from becoming a new generation of drug addicts—could be undone by these imprudent, unscientific, and flawed initiatives. These drug-legalizing initiatives are dangerous.

• *They make drug abuse more likely.* Marijuana is a "gateway" drug. Perhaps the most definitive study about the relationship between smoking marijuana, "harder" drugs and subsequent substance abuse and dependency problems is the 1994 report *Cigarettes, Alcohol, Marijuana: Gateways to Illicit Drug Use* prepared by the Center on Addiction and Substance Abuse (CASA) at Columbia University. This report found that smoking, drinking and using marijuana lead a large number of children and adults to experimentation, regular use and addiction involving substances like cocaine. Some of the key findings of the 1994 report include:

- Children who have used marijuana are more than 85 times likelier to use cocaine than children who have never used marijuana.
- The younger an individual uses any gateway drug, the more often an individual uses any gateway drug, the more gateway drugs an individual uses, the likelier that individual is to experiment with cocaine, heroin, and other illicit drugs and the likelier that individual is to become a regular adult drug user and addict.
- Sixty percent of children who smoke marijuana before age 15 move on to cocaine; only one-fifth of those who smoke marijuana after age 17 use cocaine.

• *They undermine safe medical procedures.* The regulatory procedures overseen by the Food and Drug Administration (FDA) have made the United States one of the safest countries in the world with regard to medications. A rigorous process of scientific testing is required before any drug is authorized for use by the public. Both the California and Arizona measures would bypass this proven approval process and set dangerous precedents. Scientific method, not electoral ploys, should be the basis by which we decide what is good public health policy.

• *They send the wrong message to our children.* Coming at a time that marijuana use has doubled among our youth, these initiatives threaten to undermine our efforts to prevent drug use by our children. Labeling marijuana as "medicine" sends the wrong message to children that it is a safe substance. Drug use by youngsters is even more dangerous than adult drug abuse not only because of youthful immaturity but because of ongoing physical development. Growing children may be more susceptible to neurological damage from drugs than adults because their central nervous system is still developing. Our vulnerable youth should be receiving the undiluted message that marijuana is a dangerous drug; that using it is both detrimental to one's physical and mental health.

Undesirable Effects

The therapeutic applications of smoked marijuana have been traced down to the psychoactive ingredient it contains: THC. This compound taken by mouth will relieve the vomiting resulting from cancer chemotherapy in a limited number of patients. But THC also produces acute undesirable psychic and cardiovascular symptoms, and its depressant effect on immunity is not a good indication for patients with cancer or AIDS who already have impaired immunity.

Gabriel Nahas and Nicholas A. Pace, Committees of Correspondence fact sheet, October 1994.

• *They threaten the national effort to protect our children from dangerous drugs.* Arizona's Proposition 200 seeks to okay medical use of heroin, LSD, and marijuana. Despite useful provisions such as creating a parents' commission on drug education and prevention, requiring persons who commit a violent crime while under the influence of drugs to serve 100% of their sentence, and providing for court-supervised treatment programs, the central purpose of the Arizona initiative is to strike at the very core of the system that protects all Americans from bogus medications and our children from dangerous drugs. Proposition 200 would allow doctors to prescribe drugs such as LSD, heroin, and marijuana in violation of federal law. California's Proposition 215 would allow marijuana to be smoked without a prescription and without any age limits. This loosely-worded initiative would allow Californians to obtain and use marijuana with just a physician's recommendation for any illness for which marijuana ostensibly provides relief. It also seeks to exempt those who do so from criminal prosecution or sanction. It too is in violation of federal law.

• *They are part of a wider effort to undermine our National Drug Control Strategy.* These ballot initiatives are not representative of Arizonan or Californian aspirations. They came about in large part because of the efforts of out-of-state legalizers who spent over $2 million in Arizona and California in support of both propositions. By comparison, in-state antidrug organizations raised less than $100,000 to oppose these drug legalization initiatives. Pro-drug organizations see Arizona and California as the start of what will be a state-by-state effort to overturn the policies we have developed to turn back the tide of drugs and protect our children. The initiatives are wrong: marijuana is not medicine.

No Evidence

• *No clinical evidence demonstrates that smoked marijuana is good medicine.* The National Institutes of Health (NIH) has examined all existing clinical evidence from both animal and human research in order to determine the efficacy of smoked marijuana. It has concluded that there is no clinical evidence to suggest that smoked marijuana is superior to currently available therapies for glaucoma, weight loss and wasting associated with AIDS, nausea and vomiting associated with cancer chemotherapy, muscle spasticity associated with multiple sclerosis, or intractable pain. In 1996, Health and Human Services Secretary Donna E. Shalala reiterated this conclusion in her statement that: "There is no scientifically sound evidence that smoked marijuana is medically superior to currently available therapies, including an oral prescription medication containing the active ingredient in marijuana."

• *Marijuana as medicine has been widely rejected.* Serious medical organizations as the American Medical Association, the American Cancer Society, the American Academy of Ophthalmology, and the National Multiple Sclerosis Association oppose "medical marijuana" initiatives. The National Institutes of Health—i.e., the National Eye Institute, the National Cancer Institute, the National Institute for Neurological Disorders and Stroke, the National Institute of Dental Research, and the National Institute on Allergy and Infectious Diseases—concur that there is no scientific evidence to support the use of marijuana as a medicine. National leaders such as former Surgeon General C. Everett Koop condemned the Arizona and California propositions as did former Presidents Gerald Ford, Jimmy Carter, and George Bush. President Bill Clinton and Vice President Al Gore are firm in their opposition to these legalization initiatives. The anecdotal information about the supposed medicinal benefits of marijuana offered by the backers of these proposals has not convinced those who base their conclusions on scientific fact.

THE MANY HARMS OF MARIJUANA

• *Smoked marijuana is harmful.* NIH scientists are also concerned that smoked marijuana could be harmful to people with impaired immune systems, particularly AIDS patients, who are susceptible to lung infections such as pneumocystis pneumonia. NIH is further concerned that smoking marijuana is significantly associated with bacterial pneumonia among HIV-infected individuals. Secretary Shalala shares these concerns. She has stated that: "There is clear scientific evidence that marijuana is harmful to one's brain, heart, and lungs. It limits learning, memory, perception, judgment, and complex motor skills like those needed to drive a vehicle. It has been shown to damage motivation and interest in one's goals and activities. It can cause chronic coughing and bronchitis. In short, it is a very dangerous drug."

• *Alternative therapies are adequate.* The principal active ingredient in marijuana is delta-9- Tetrahydrocannabinol (THC). Purified, synthetic THC is known as dronabinol and is marketed under the trade name Marinol. Marinol is commercially available as an antiemetic for cancer patients and to treat anorexia associated with weight loss in patients with AIDS. Other drugs and treatments are available for the conditions smoked marijuana would ostensibly ameliorate, including 24 drugs approved by the FDA for glaucoma and many for nausea associated with cancer chemotherapy and chronic pain. Many of these drugs are considered superior to marijuana in effectiveness and safety. Because these oral medications are free of the contaminants found in smoked marijuana, they do not harm the lungs, heart, and immune system the way that smoked marijuana does. . . .

NO ACCEPTED MEDICAL USE

• *Marijuana should remain a "Schedule I" drug.* Congress has prohibited the general availability of marijuana for use as medicine by placing it in Schedule I of the federal Controlled Substances Act. This federal law of 1970 schedules drugs according to their effects, medical use, and potential for abuse. Schedule I drugs are those defined as having "a high potential for abuse . . . no currently accepted medical use in treatment in the United States . . . [and] a lack of accepted safety for use of the drug or other substance under medical supervision." Other Schedule I drugs include heroin, LSD, hashish, methaqualone, and designer drugs. The law further provides that to place marijuana in Schedule II (as cocaine is) or in a lower schedule, there must be a finding that it has a "currently accepted medical use in treatment in the United States. . . ." The Department of Health and Human Services knows of no medical or scientific evidence that suggests a re- evaluation of the scheduling of marijuana under federal law. Drug Enforcement Administrator Thomas A. Constantine firmly opposes a rescheduling of marijuana "because there is no evidence that marijuana is an effective medical treatment." He also asks "at a time when our nation is looking for solutions to the problem of teenage drug use, how can we justify giving a stamp of approval to an illegal substance which has no legitimate medical use?"

FUTURE RESEARCH

• *Further research should be considered.* Established federal policy is to treat research on the therapeutic use of marijuana the same as research on any other drug of abuse potential. Neither the FDA nor the National Institutes of Health are opposed to controlled and well-conducted clinical trials or studies for any drug including marijuana. The FDA would of course follow regulations governing the use in humans of investigational new drug substances and the requirements for approval of a new medication. As with all controlled substances, therapeutic marijuana would be subject to all of the stipulations of the U.S. Controlled Substances Act. This act requires an application be registered with the Drug Enforcement Administration. This is a process independent from FDA's review and would be required in order for clinical studies to proceed. There is presently no clinical evidence to suggest that marijuana leaf should be permitted to become the first U.S. Food and Drug Administration-approved medicine in the form of a cigarette.

• *We must continue to uphold our federal laws.* Drug use and its consequences have gone down in large part because of the efforts of federal, state, and local law enforcement agencies. Upholding our laws has been and must continue to be an essential component of our drug control strategy. Deputy Assistant Attorney General Mary Lee Warren affirmed this principle to Los Angeles County Sheriff Brad Gates: "It should be clear, however, that, whatever the applicable state law, those who distribute or use marijuana act in violation of federal law and are therefore subject to federal prosecution."

| "Medical nutrition therapy should be
an integral part of the ongoing
health care of people with HIV."

AIDS SHOULD BE TREATED WITH MEDICAL NUTRITION THERAPY

American Dietetic Association and Canadian Dietetic Association

In the following viewpoint, the American Dietetic Association and the Canadian Dietetic Association argue that medical nutrition therapy and education should be a vital component of the health care of people with HIV and AIDS. Such intervention, the associations assert, is necessary to provide patients with essential nutrients and to prevent weight loss and infection. The associations are organizations of dietetic professionals who promote optimal nutrition.

As you read, consider the following questions:

1. What deficiencies affect the immune system and other body functions, according to the associations?
2. According to the associations, what percentage of AIDS patients will experience wasting syndrome?
3. Why must the issue of food safety be discussed with all HIV/AIDS patients, in the authors' opinion?

Excerpted from "Position of the American Dietetic Association and the Canadian Dietetic Association: Nutrition Intervention in the Care of Persons with Human Immunodeficiency Virus Infection," *Journal of the American Dietetic Association*, vol. 94 (1994), pp. 1,042-45; *http://www.eatright.org/positions.html*. Reprinted by permission of the American Dietetic Association.

Immune dysfunction resulting from infection with the human immunodeficiency virus (HIV) has become a major health threat to populations in the United States, Canada, and throughout the world. As HIV-infected persons survive previously life-threatening infection through the use of effective medical therapies, malnutrition and wasting have become central issues in the health care plan of longer-term survivors. Medical nutrition therapy should be an integral part of the ongoing health care of people with HIV. Medical nutrition therapy involves an assessment of nutritional status and treatment. Treatment includes diet therapy, counseling, or use of specialized nutrition supplements (nutrition support by mouth, tube, or vein). Research about the relationship between nutrition and HIV infection is essential for understanding the mechanisms of wasting and for determining the effectiveness of medical nutrition therapy.

Since the early 1980s, many health care professionals have recognized acquired immunodeficiency syndrome (AIDS) as a major health care problem. The etiologic agent of AIDS is HIV, which attacks the immune system, rendering a person susceptible to infection and neoplasm. D.C. Macallan et al. and M.K. Hellerstein et al. point out that the malnutrition often seen with AIDS is a result of metabolic processes both usual for other chronic and acute diseases and unique to HIV disease. Malnutrition and its complications can further render an HIV-infected person susceptible to opportunistic infections and reduce the effectiveness of and tolerance to medications and therapies. Thus, patients and the health care team should pay special attention to the prevention and treatment of malnutrition and wasting in HIV disease.

It is the position of The American Dietetic Association and The Canadian Dietetic Association that nutrition intervention—medical nutrition therapy—and education should be components of the total health care provided to persons infected with the human immunodeficiency virus.

The Impact of HIV

The impact of HIV disease in the United States and Canada includes psychosocial and financial consequences. . . . The Centers for Disease Control and Prevention estimates that approximately 1 million people, or one in every 250 people in the United States, are infected with HIV. The life-threatening acute and chronic diseases that are related to HIV infection present the health care delivery system with unknown challenges.

Health care providers are quickly learning new therapies and methods of treating HIV and AIDS. In addition, they are dealing with an array of cultural and lifestyle differences in the people infected and affected by HIV. Trends suggest that the rate of HIV infection is growing in women, adolescents, children, intravenous drug users, the incarcerated, and the poor and homeless. Cost of care for HIV-infected persons is seen as an extreme burden on health care systems. The increased costs of HIV/AIDS care are associated primarily with hospitalization. Cost-containment strategies for HIV health care include preventive efforts and timely, effective treatments for complications of opportunistic infection and neoplasm. Prevention and prompt, effective treatment of opportunistic infection are the first line of defense against rapid weight loss and lean body mass loss seen with HIV and AIDS.

NUTRITION AND HIV INTERACTION

Researchers have explored the effects of HIV and its complications on nutritional status, and the effect of an individual's nutritional well-being on the process and progress of the disease. Researchers have established that deficiencies of energy, protein, and micronutrients adversely affect the immune system and other normal body functions. R.T. Chlebowski et al. suggested that nutritional status may be a major determinant of survival. Adequate protein stores and micronutrient status are necessary for the effectiveness of many drug therapies. For example, doxorubicin hydrochloride, an antineoplastic drug, requires adequate riboflavin status to reduce drug toxicity.

An estimated 80% or more of AIDS patients will experience the adverse effects of wasting syndrome. Weight loss is often used as the first indicator of nutritional compromise in clinical settings. However, because changes in body composition may occur regardless of weight maintenance, and are often present throughout all stages of HIV disease, weight loss may not be a good early indication of the risk for malnutrition.

Hellerstein and D.P. Kotler et al. discussed the cascade of events that occurs as part of immune response to infection and that results in preferential and rapid lean body mass wasting in people infected with HIV. In a New York study, Kotler et al. demonstrated the relationship between the degree of lean tissue wasting and mortality in people with AIDS. Death occurred at approximately 54% of normal body cell mass. Yet some research suggests that weight loss may not be an inevitable part of the disease process.

Malnutrition may also affect disease process and progress.

Laboratory values and their reflection of nutritional status are important prognostic indicators in HIV disease. Malnutrition exacerbates immune dysfunction and contributes to the deterioration of a patient's quality of life and ability to carry out the activities of daily living. Kotler speculated that by reversing the malnutrition that often accompanies HIV disease, a patient may experience an improved level of functioning in activities of daily living, clinical well-being, and longer-term survival. B. Abrams et al. reported a 31% reduction in progression to an AIDS-defining diagnosis for patients regularly consuming a multivitamin/mineral supplement. . . .

NUTRITIONAL STATUS SCREENING AND ASSESSMENT

Screening for the risk of malnutrition is an important step in early intervention to prevent wasting of lean body mass. Initial nutrition screening can be conducted by a health care professional, support service volunteer, the patient's family or friends, or the patient. The registered dietitian must help health care providers and others identify risk factors and indicators for malnutrition.

Identification of any risk factors or indicators for malnutrition should be followed by a full nutrition assessment conducted by a registered dietitian. The purpose of establishing clinical profiles of patients (i.e., a summary of parameters affecting clinical well-being) is to determine the potential reasons for risk or indication of malnutrition and to suggest the most effective nutrition interventions. A complete nutrition assessment includes a review of medical history and risk factors; a medication profile; a nutritional profile; a biochemical evaluation; notation of psychosocial and economic conditions and prognosis; and development of a medical care plan.

The complete nutrition assessment should help the registered dietitian determine and prioritize appropriate nutrition interventions. Rehabilitation efforts with nutrition supplements alone have been less than satisfactory. Nutrition, medication, and exercise should be integrated into the medical care to protect and restore optimal nutritional stores.

NUTRITION CARE PLANNING

Strategies for nutrition care should specifically address risk factors or other problems (such as inadequate food access, decreased nutrient intake, and body composition changes) identified by the nutritional status screen and assessments. The registered dietitian needs to establish realistic and individualized goals to meet the nutrition needs identified. The nutrition goals should align with the goals of the overall health care plan, as determined jointly by the health care team and the person with HIV/AIDS. The health care team can provide support to the patient by reinforcing the nutrition goals and strategies, and can provide the registered dietitian with feedback on the patient's progress. The nutrition care plan requires monitoring and may need ongoing adjustment to parallel changes in the overall health care plan and to meet the patient's changing needs.

In developing a nutrition care plan, the registered dietitian needs to consider:

(a) the feasibility of nutritional repletion
(b) patient prognosis and desire for well-being
(c) the medical treatment plan
(d) the health care setting (i.e., acute, long-term, home care, or outpatient) in which the nutrition care will be provided.

Desirable nutrition-related outcomes may include preservation of lean body tissue, improvement in quality of life, and/or tolerance to medications/treatments. Documentation and evaluation are important components of the nutrition care plan.

NUTRITION EDUCATION AND COUNSELING

Specific counseling guidelines and nutrition education recommendations have been suggested. Nutrition education should address the following areas:

- Healthful eating principles (what nutrients are important and why, use of vitamin mineral supplements, frequency of eating)
- Healthful eating plan (what to eat and recommended amounts)
- Food-safety issues (food storage, food preparation, dining away from home)
- Managing nutrition-related symptoms (how to deal with poor appetite, early satiety, nausea/vomiting, diarrhea, food intolerances, mouth sores, swallowing difficulties, and fever)
- Alternative feeding methods (use of nutritional supplements, tube feeding, or parenteral nutrition support)
- Guidelines for evaluating nutrition information and products (special diet plans, individual vitamin/mineral supplements or other suggested nutrition practices).

All of the aforementioned nutrition education topics are important, but the issue of food safety must be addressed with every patient with HIV/AIDS because of their increased susceptibility to foodborne illness. Also, the registered dietitian needs to address how the patient can evaluate various nutrition-related alternative therapies because people with HIV/AIDS are susceptible to nutrition misinformation. Providing a set of guidelines for evaluating nutrition information can help patients make their own decisions regarding the use of nutrition-related alternatives.

PROTEIN REQUIREMENTS

HIV status does change protein requirements: We need two-to-three times over the levels required for HIV-negative counterparts. High protein foods include meat, fish, poultry, eggs and dairy. Vegetarian food patterns for protein may still allow milk, yogurt and/or eggs, possibly fish, and also tofu, legumes (beans, peas, lentils), grains, nuts and seeds.

Jennifer Jensen, *Alive & Kicking!*, January 1996.

A number of researchers have assessed the effectiveness of dietary counseling on the nutritional status of the people with HIV/AIDS. Authors of these studies suggest that intensive counseling and the selective use of oral nutritional supplements can be an effective intervention. Therefore, nutrition education and counseling provided by a registered dietitian are key elements of health care for persons with HIV.

NUTRITION SUPPORT STRATEGIES

At some point in the progression of HIV, aggressive nutrition support may need to be implemented. In patients who are nutritionally compromised despite adequate food intake and absorption, the health care team must explore the possibility that the patient has an altered metabolism or an underlying infection. In comparing the current caloric intake to the estimated needs, energy expenditures of patients with HIV/AIDS may be higher than standard estimates. However, increased energy expenditures may not adequately explain the caloric deficit leading to weight loss or lean body mass loss. Opportunistic infections will alter the metabolism of nutrients regardless of food intake and absorption.

If the patient is able to absorb adequate nutrients but is unable to ingest adequate amounts of foods and oral nutritional supplements, then enteral or parenteral nutrition support should be considered. If absorption is adequate, tube feeding may provide an adjunctive or alternative to the oral route. Modifications in diet and/or use of specialty formulas may provide adequate nutrient composition while helping the patient overcome mild to moderate malabsorption. Complications of severe malabsorption, copious diarrhea, or other factors that prohibit use of enteral feedings may justify the use of parenteral feeding for total or adjunctive nutrient administration depending on the goals of the therapy. In any case, decisions regarding the use of enteral and parenteral nutrition should comply with the patient's expressed consent.

Because malnutrition is caused by a number of factors, rehabilitation from malnutrition requires a multitherapy approach. Rehabilitation and prevention of malnutrition share many elements, especially an emphasis on building of lean body mass. In addition to the provision of adequate nutrition via oral, enteral, or parenteral routes, exercise may become an essential component of therapy to improve lean body mass. Increased activity levels may improve the patient's stamina and ability to perform the resistance exercises that are required to build and maintain lean body mass.

DRUG AND NUTRIENT INTERACTION

Persons with HIV commonly take more than one or two drugs for prophylaxis, maintenance, and/or treatment of opportunistic infection and neoplasm. Additional risk of nutritional compromise because of multiple drug therapies can be secondary to the potential for increased numbers of side effects, nutrient alterations, and drug-drug interactions. The registered dietitian needs to monitor for potential drug-nutrient interactions and develop nutrition interventions to combat possible side effects such as anorexia, nausea/vomiting, or diarrhea. Specific nutrition recommendations should be based on the patient's nutritional profile with consideration to a risk vs. benefit analysis for each individual. The addition or use of special forms of macronutrient and micronutrient supplements may be beneficial to combat nutritional losses attributable to drug-nutrient interactions. However, the benefits should be weighed against the burdens, such as costs or compromises to quality of life.

The goals of medical nutrition therapy in HIV disease include early assessment and treatment of nutrient deficiencies, maintenance and restoration of lean body mass, and support for activities of daily living and quality of life. The maintenance and restoration of nutritional stores are closely interrelated and interdependent with each of the other recommended medical therapies. Therefore, it is vital to the health of persons with HIV/AIDS to have access to the services of a registered dietitian, who is the essential member of the health care team for providing medical nutrition therapy. The registered dietitian should take an active role in developing nutrition care protocols for HIV/AIDS in their practice setting. Dietetics professionals must take responsibility for obtaining and maintaining current knowledge in this area and should take the lead in translating current knowledge and research into practical and realistic nutrition guidelines for persons with HIV/AIDS.

Further research is needed in the area of HIV/AIDS and nutrition. Registered dietitians and other members of the health care team are encouraged to conduct nutrition research in the area of nutrition interventions and the outcomes of nutrition therapy. Additionally, government health-related agencies, national AIDS-related organizations, and private industry should be encouraged to provide funding sources and support to the issue of research in nutrition-related problems and interventions in HIV/AIDS.

> "It behooves the individual to bring in many therapies, and Chinese medicine is a very useful option."

CHINESE THERAPIES CAN HELP AIDS PATIENTS

Thomas M. Sinclair, interviewed by John S. James

Thomas M. Sinclair is the executive director of the Immune Enhancement Project, a San Francisco clinic that provides Chinese therapies to patients with HIV and other illnesses. The following viewpoint is excerpted from an interview of Sinclair by John S. James, the editor in chief of the biweekly newsletter *AIDS Treatment News*. Sinclair argues that Chinese therapies, including acupuncture, herbal treatments, and relaxation exercises, can be effective treatments for people with HIV. The patients who react best to Chinese therapies, Sinclair contends, are those who start treatment in the early stage of their infection and those who get consistent treatment.

As you read, consider the following questions:

1. What is an herbal decoction, according to Sinclair?
2. In Sinclair's opinion, what does the sensation of chi signify?
3. According to Sinclair, what do patients gain from performing Qigong and Tai Chi?

Excerpted from Thomas M. Sinclair, "Using Acupuncture in the Treatment of AIDS," an interview of Thomas M. Sinclair by John S. James, *AIDS Treatment News*, September 1, 1995. Reprinted by permission.

John S. James: *Where do you have most success with traditional Chinese medicine, and where does it not work as well?*

Thomas M. Sinclair: Traditional Chinese medicine has been particularly successful in treating peripheral neuropathy, sinusitis, pain-related problems, night sweats, insomnia, dry skin, headache, and low energy and fatigue.

With digestive problems, we do not always get a person functioning back at a normal level. But often acupuncture, together with diet changes or medication, can help to return the digestion to a more normal state.

What has not worked well? The first condition that comes to mind has been Kaposi's sarcoma (KS). We have not had good success in that area.

And sometimes in late-stage AIDS it is difficult to make dramatic changes, as the body's energy is so depleted.

ACUPUNCTURE, HERBS, AND OTHER TREATMENTS

Should patients usually take acupuncture and herbal treatments together?

When I work with patients, I like to work with both. Often I will work on a more long-term, internal basis using herbs. They come in decoctions (prepared into a drink like a strong tea), or tinctures (herbal extracts in alcohol), or raw compressed tablets. Often they have a slower effect than acupuncture, but act better over a long time. Often I will use the acupuncture treatment for immediate symptom relief.

If someone comes in with a headache, or neuropathy, or sinusitis, I will probably use acupuncture to treat those symptoms. But the underlying condition, the HIV infection, we would probably treat more with herbs. This rule has many exceptions, of course, in how I work with people.

I think it's best to use both herbs and acupuncture together. But some people have certain preferences. Some have a fear of needles, or have had bad experiences, or just do not find acupuncture pleasant; there is nothing wrong with just using the herbs. And some people do not like taking herbs; particularly in HIV infection, people are taking so many pills, and one of the problems with the herbs is that you need to take a lot of product to have an effect—simply because there is a lot of fiber. Look for a practitioner who is flexible, to work with you where you're at.

Can you describe herbal decoctions?

That is the traditional way of taking herbs in China. They put together a formula by assembling many loose herbs, as roots, barks, seeds, twigs, berries; then that mixture is cooked, and the liquid is reduced, and drunk over a period of time.

Is acupuncture painful?

That is a concern for many people. Of course you feel a prick as the needle penetrates the skin. What people sometimes describe as painful is more the acupuncture needling sensation; it's the arrival of chi (also spelled qi) at that point. That can feel like a burning, a tingling, numbness, a grabbing sensation, an electric sensation. This is an appropriate response; it's what we are looking for. It means that your body is responding to the stimulation it is receiving.

Most people find acupuncture sessions very relaxing, whatever we treat. Some patients just have a great sensitivity; usually people are much more sensitive when they first start treatment. As your body becomes more balanced and more adjusted, you will find that the needling sensations are much less painful.

EARLY AND CONSISTENT TREATMENT

How often does one receive acupuncture?

What I have observed in eight years of treating persons with HIV with herbs and acupuncture is that those who do the best are those who start early, and those who are very consistent. How often you see a practitioner can depend on your lifestyle, your economic situation, your commitments. The best thing is to be very regular; it may be once a month, twice a month, twice a week—what is important is to stay with it over a long period of time. I often tell clients I would rather they come in once a month for three years than once a week for three months. Treatment with herbs and acupuncture is a subtle process which can have dramatic changes, but you need to think about the long haul.

As Westerners, as members of a pill-popping society, people want to have immediate results. Of course we try to achieve that, but you have to temper this goal with the realization that Chinese medicine is a long-term therapy. If you are going to do it, to get the best results, think of the long term.

Can you explain other procedures, such as moxibustion, or electrical stimulation of acupuncture points, or qigong?

In California our license covers the use of herbs, acupuncture, and related methods including electric stimulation, the application of cups (basically creating a kind of suction on the body), and the burning of mugwort (which is called moxibustion).

Often moxibustion is used extensively with HIV. Chinese medicine looks at the influence of environmental factors, such as heat, cold, dampness, wind; often, temperature in the body is very important. In HIV we often see a deficiency, where the body's energy is very low, the tongue might have a white coat, digestion might be poor, there could be diarrhea. One of the treatments for that is the use of moxibustion, or the burning of mugwort over acupuncture points. The whole idea here is to put energy into the body, feed energy into a weak and deficient system.

THE MAGIC OF ORIENTAL MEDICINE

As a treatment choice for those people who are immunocompromised, acupuncture and Traditional Oriental Medicine are excellent because treatment takes place at the mental, the emotional, and the spiritual, as well as the physical, level. Indeed, one of the most enjoyable examples of feedback I've received from a person was the statement: "I feel well; I had forgotten what that was like; I thought I'd never feel well again."

This is the magic of Traditional Oriental Medicine: by teaching a person it is possible to feel well as a result of receiving acupuncture, the person comes to understand that a return to health is an accessible option.

Christopher Huson, *Seattle AIDS Treatment Project Newsletter*, Spring 1996.

Practitioners use moxibustion in different ways. They may put the moxi on an acupuncture needle and burn it. They may burn a stick of moxi over the needling site. There are other methods, such as applying moxi onto a piece of aconite which is placed directly on the body.

And electrical stimulation?

Often we use that for pain relief; it's a modern development in acupuncture. We get very good results, particularly with conditions like neuropathy, through the use of electrical stimulations.

CHINESE AND WESTERN MEDICINE

How do you integrate Eastern and Western care?

Since 1990 we have seen a tremendous change in physician attitudes. It used to go from indifference to outright hostility; now there is more acceptance and, in fact, encouragement of the integration of care.

My philosophy on HIV is to use whatever you can get your hands on that is consistent with your belief system. That might not be acupuncture—it might be yoga or spiritual work, or meditation, or strictly pharmaceuticals and drug trials. There is no one right way with HIV, especially given the chronic nature of the disease—and the limitations of Western medicines. Western medicines often have an impact on opportunistic infections, but in terms of stopping the underlying process, I don't think medical science has achieved that yet. It behooves the individual to bring in many therapies, and Chinese medicine is a very useful option.

It's important that you have a good working relationship with your physician, and it's even more important that your physician supports your integrating Chinese medicine, herbs and acupuncture into your treatment program.

If you are having trouble with neuropathy, for example, there is no entirely satisfactory Western medication to treat it; doctors have amitriptyline and a few other drugs. The physician could refer you to acupuncture to treat the neuropathy, which may be induced by drugs like d4T or ddI or ddC; that is a valuable synthesis right there. Or if you have digestive upset, you might have parasite cultures, an endoscopy, sigmoidoscopy—standard Western procedures. They may not identify a pathogen; then you may choose to treat with Chinese medicine. This is another opportunity to integrate both models.

The question comes up about the use of AZT, 3TC, or other antivirals. Here I come back to the philosophy that you need to use everything you can to stay healthy and stay alive. I used to feel that if one pill is good, ten pills is much better. I'm coming to see that an important principle with HIV is to use the minimum amount of treatment to achieve the maximum effect. I have seen people come into this clinic who are on Neupogen and Procrit because they have poor bone marrow reserves; they are combining ganciclovir, hydroxyurea, multiple nucleosides, and they wonder why they have problems with bone marrow.

RELAXATION TECHNIQUES

What is "Qigong"—and how does it relate to "Tai Chi," a term more familiar to our readers?

Both are variations of each other. Each is a systematic series of movements that serve to enhance the body's energy. Qigong tends to be slower; it is less of a martial art. Tai Chi can be a defensive martial art, even though it also is gentle and soothing.

Each gives one a profound sense of relaxation. What I hear constantly from our clients who do Qigong or Tai Chi is that they have increased energy. It does not take a lot of technology or training to learn the basic form; then it's up to you to practice.

You mentioned that the practitioner can act as client advocate, can help the client be informed about lifestyle, diet, stress, and alternative/complementary treatments. Can you give some examples?

I look at the relationship between the practitioner of Chinese medicine and the client as a prevention strategy. Particularly with a well-trained practitioner, they can recognize early danger signs. For example, in this clinic, we have seen patients come in with a splitting headache, they are sensitive to light, they have a stiff neck—these are signs of meningitis. A number of times we have referred people immediately to the emergency room. Sometimes we will treat, and then have the patient call their physician, or go into the emergency room to be treated.

Patients usually see their acupuncturist much more frequently than they see their Western physician. It is important that you pick a practitioner who is experienced, so he or she can be a sentinel for early danger signs, and knows when to refer you to a Western provider.

The relationship that develops is often intimate, informal. It's a good opportunity for the practitioner to talk to you about lifestyle decisions you are making: stress, coffee, activity, exercise, drug use. Acupuncture has an aspect of disease prevention; certainly we see that in the reduction of colds and flu. If we accept the theory that you want to prevent the immune system from being stimulated (to avoid stimulating the growth of HIV), Chinese medicine may have a beneficial effect.

HIV can be very overwhelming; it is difficult for people to make a lot of choices. A well-informed practitioner can talk to you about clinical trials, about Western medications, about other alternative therapies, about nutrients and supplements.

PERIODICAL BIBLIOGRAPHY

The following articles have been selected to supplement the diverse views presented in this chapter. Addresses are provided for periodicals not indexed in the *Readers' Guide to Periodical Literature*, the *Alternative Press Index*, the *Social Sciences Index*, or the *Index to Legal Periodicals and Books*.

Mike Barr	"Attack of the Mutation Monster," POZ, August/September 1996. Available from LLC, 349 W. Twelfth St., New York, NY 10014-1721.
Mike Barr	"The Morning After," POZ, February 1997.
John G. Bartlett	"Conquering HIV," *World & I*, June 1996. Available from 3600 New York Ave. NE, Washington, DC 20002.
Lawrence Corey and King K. Holmes	"Therapy for Human Immunodeficiency Virus Infection: What Have We Learned?" *New England Journal of Medicine*, October 10, 1996. Available from 1440 Main St., Waltham, MA 02154-0413.
John Gallagher	"HIV: Hiding in Plain Sight," *Advocate*, March 18, 1997.
Nancy Knoblock Hunton	"All Natural AIDS Protection?" *Technology Review*, August/September 1996.
JAMA	Issue on AIDS and treatment, July 10, 1996. Available from AMA, 535 N. Dearborn St., Chicago, IL 60610.
Jerome P. Kassirer	"Federal Foolishness and Marijuana," *New England Journal of Medicine*, January 30, 1997.
Michael H. Merson	"How to Fight AIDS," *Newsweek*, August 5, 1996.
Shari Roan	"Diagnosis: Hope," *Los Angeles Times*, April 16, 1997. Available from Reprints, Times Mirror Square, Los Angeles, CA 90053.
Rebecca Voelker	"Can Researchers Use New Drugs to Push HIV Envelope to Extinction?" *JAMA*, August 14, 1996.

FOR FURTHER DISCUSSION

CHAPTER 1

1. John S. James and Gabriel Rotello disagree about the potential of protease inhibitors to combat the AIDS crisis. Whose argument is more persuasive? Why? On what aspect of HIV do the authors agree?

2. In his viewpoint, Max Essex contends that new HIV epidemics could strike heterosexuals in Europe and North America. Peter W. Plumley argues that the risk of a healthy heterosexual contracting HIV is "one-in-a-million." Which author's viewpoint most strongly influences your opinion about the spread of HIV? Explain.

CHAPTER 2

1. Helen Mathews Smith argues that routine testing for HIV is necessary in order to track and contain the virus. The American Civil Liberties Union asserts that mandatory testing violates the constitutional right to privacy. Based on the viewpoints in the chapter, do you think testing for the AIDS virus should be voluntary or mandatory? Explain your answer.

2. According to William O. Fabbri, home test kits for HIV would encourage many people to test themselves for the AIDS virus and would result in a lower infection rate because HIV-positive people would take precautions to reduce the spread of AIDS. Christopher J. Portelli maintains, however, that the risks associated with home test kits would outweigh the benefits. Which argument do you think is more convincing? Why?

3. Geoffrey A.D. Smereck advocates partner notification, or contact tracing, as a means of controlling the spread of HIV. Mark S. Senak contends, however, that such a policy would be impractical. Based on your reading of the viewpoints in this chapter, do you think contact tracing would reduce the spread of AIDS? Why or why not?

CHAPTER 3

1. The Centers for Disease Control and Prevention maintains that condoms, when used correctly, are an effective means of preventing the transmission of HIV. According to Anthony Zimmerman, however, promoting the use of condoms to prevent AIDS will lead to promiscuity, which will increase the likelihood of contracting the fatal disease. In your opinion, will the advocacy of condom usage reduce or increase the spread of AIDS? Explain your answer.

2. Needle exchange programs (NEPs) are an effective means of controlling the spread of AIDS, according to Peter Lurie and Pamela DeCarlo. But Mitchell S. Rosenthal and Joseph Farah contend that NEPs are based on questionable assumptions, do nothing to slow the transmission of HIV via sexual intercourse, and implicitly condone drug use. Which argument do you think is stronger? Why?

3. James Loyce, Walt Odets, and John Gagnon debate the merits of various AIDS education programs in reducing risky behavior for those at risk of contracting HIV. Do you think AIDS education programs are effective in changing risky behavior? Why or why not? If not, how can these programs be made more effective, in your opinion? Use examples from the viewpoints to support your reasoning.

CHAPTER 4

1. How do Jerome Groopman and Jeffrey L. Reynolds differ in their descriptions of the drug AZT? How do these descriptions compare to their opinions about protease inhibitors? Explain your answers.

2. Kevin B. Zeese is the president of the public policy organization Common Sense for Drug Policy. Barry R. McCaffrey directs the federal Office of National Drug Control Policy. How are the authors' backgrounds evident in their views of medical marijuana? Which of these viewpoints is more convincing, and why? Does knowing the authors' backgrounds influence your assessment of their arguments? If so, in what way?

ORGANIZATIONS TO CONTACT

The editors have compiled the following list of organizations concerned with the issues debated in this book. The descriptions are derived from materials provided by the organizations. All have publications or information available for interested readers. The list was compiled on the date of publication of the present volume; names, addresses, phone and fax numbers, and e-mail and Internet addresses may change. Be aware that many organizations take several weeks or longer to respond to inquiries, so allow as much time as possible.

American Civil Liberties Union (ACLU)
125 Broad St., 18th Fl., New York, NY 10004
(212) 944-9800 • Internet: http://www.aclu.org
The ACLU is the nation's oldest and largest civil liberties organization. Its Lesbian and Gay Rights/AIDS Project, started in 1986, handles litigation, education, and public policy work on behalf of gays and lesbians. It publishes the handbook *The Rights of Lesbians and Gay Men*.

American Foundation for AIDS Research (AmFAR)
733 Third Ave., 12th Fl., New York, NY 10097
(212) 682-7440 • fax: (212) 682-9812
Internet: http://www.amfar.org
The American Foundation for AIDS Research supports AIDS prevention and research and advocates AIDS-related public policy. It publishes several monographs, compendiums, journals, and periodic publications, including the *AIDS/HIV Treatment Directory*, published twice a year, the newsletter *HIV/AIDS Educator and Reporter*, published three times a year, and the quarterly *AmFAR Newsletter*.

American Red Cross AIDS Education Office
1709 New York Ave. NW, Suite 208, Washington, DC 20006
(202) 434-4074 • e-mail: info@usa.redcross.org
Internet: http://www.redcross.org
Established in 1881, the American Red Cross is one of America's oldest public health organizations. Its AIDS Education Office publishes pamphlets, brochures, and posters containing facts about AIDS. These materials are available at local Red Cross chapters. In addition, many chapters offer informational videotapes, conduct presentations, and operate speakers' bureaus.

Center for Women Policy Studies (CWPS)
1211 Connecticut Ave. NW, Suite 312, Washington, DC 20036
(202) 872-1770 • fax: (202) 296-8962
e-mail: HN4066@handsnet.org
The CWPS was the first national policy institute to focus specifically on issues affecting the social, legal, and economic status of women. It believes that the government and the medical community have neglected

the effect of AIDS on women and that more action should be taken to help women who have AIDS. The center publishes the book *The Guide to Resources on Women and AIDS* and produces the video *Fighting for Our Lives: Women Confronting AIDS.*

Centers for Disease Control and Prevention (CDC)
National AIDS Clearinghouse
PO Box 6003, Rockville, MD 20849-6003
(800) 458-5231 • fax: (301) 738-6616
e-mail: aidsinfo@cdcnac.org • Internet: http://www.cdcnac.org
The CDC is the government agency charged with protecting the public health of the nation by preventing and controlling diseases and by responding to public health emergencies. The CDC National AIDS Clearinghouse is a reference, referral, and distribution service for HIV/AIDS-related information. All of the clearinghouse's services are designed to facilitate the sharing of information and resources among people working in HIV prevention, treatment, and support services. The CDC publishes information about AIDS in the *HIV/AIDS Prevention Newsletter*, and it includes updates on the disease in its *Morbidity and Mortality Weekly Report.*

Family Research Council
700 13th St. NW, Suite 500, Washington DC 20005
(202) 393-2100 • fax: (202) 393-2134
e-mail: corrdept@frc.org • Internet: http://www.frc.org
The Family Research Council promotes the traditional family unit and the Judeo-Christian value system. The council opposes the public education system's tolerance of homosexuality and condom distribution programs, which its members believe encourage sexual promiscuity and lead to the spread of AIDS. It publishes numerous reports from a conservative perspective, including the monthly newsletter *Washington Watch*, the bimonthly journal *Family Policy*, and *Free to Be Family*, a 1992 report that addresses issues such as pornography, sex education, sexually transmitted diseases, and teen sex.

Focus on the Family
8605 Explorer Dr., Colorado Springs, CO 80995
(719) 531-3400 • (800) A-FAMILY (232-6459) • fax: (719) 548-4525
Internet: http://harvest.reapernet.com/fof/page18.html
Focus on the Family promotes Christian values and strong family ties and campaigns against pornography and homosexual rights laws. It publishes the monthly magazines *Focus on the Family* and *Focus on the Family Citizen* for parents, children, and educators as well as the video *Sex, Lies, and . . . the Truth*, which encourages abstinence and criticizes safe-sex methods, which its members believe increase the spread of AIDS. Publications are available from its Internet website.

Gay Men's Health Crisis

Publications/Education Dept.

119 W. 24th St., New York, NY 10011-0022

(212) 337-1950 • fax: (212) 367-1220 • TTY: (212) 645-7470

Internet: http://www.gmhc.org

Founded in 1982, the Gay Men's Health Crisis provides support services, education, and advocacy for men, women, and children with AIDS. The group produces the cable television news show *Living with AIDS* and publishes *Treatment Issues*, a monthly newsletter that discusses experimental AIDS therapies, the *Treatment Fact Sheets*, the periodical newsletters *Lesbian AIDS Project* and *Notes*, and various brochures.

Harvard AIDS Institute

651 Huntington Ave., Boston, MA 02115

(617) 432-4400 • fax: (617) 432-4545

The Harvard AIDS Institute is a university-wide organization that promotes the understanding of HIV prevention, transmission, diagnosis, and treatment. It also works to advance AIDS education on local, national, and international levels; to provide multidisciplinary AIDS training to scientists and clinicians throughout the world; and to stimulate the development of policies and solutions that benefit those affected by the HIV epidemic. The institute publishes the newsletter *Harvard AIDS Review* twice a year.

National AIDS Fund

1730 K St. NW, Suite 815, Washington, DC 20006

(202) 408-4848 • Internet: http://www.aidsfund.org

The National AIDS Fund seeks to eliminate HIV as a major health and social problem. Its members work in partnership with the public and private sectors to provide care and to prevent new infections in communities and in the workplace by means of advocacy, grants, research, and education. The fund publishes the monthly newsletter *News from the National AIDS Fund*, which is also available through their website.

National Association of People with AIDS (NAPWA)

1413 K St. NW, Washington, DC 20005-3442

(202) 898-0414 • fax: (202) 898-0435

e-mail: napwa@thecure.org • Internet: http://www.thecure.org

NAPWA is an organization that represents people with HIV. Its members believe that it is the inalienable right of every person with HIV to have health care, to be free from discrimination, to have the right to a dignified death, to be adequately housed, to be protected from violence, and to travel and immigrate regardless of country of origin or HIV status. The association publishes several informational materials such as an annual strategic agenda and the annual *Community Report*.

National Institute of Allergies and Infectious Diseases (NIAID)
Office of Communications
Bldg. 31, Rm. 7A-50, 31 Center Dr., MSC 2520, Bethesda, MD 20892-2520
(301) 496-5717 • fax: (301) 402-0120
Internet: http://www.niaid.nih.org
NIAID, a component of the National Institutes of Health, supports research aimed at preventing, diagnosing, and treating diseases such as AIDS and tuberculosis as well as allergic conditions like asthma. NIAID publishes educational materials, including the booklet *Understanding the Immune System* and fact sheets describing AIDS drug and vaccine development and the effect of AIDS on women, children, and minority populations.

People with AIDS Coalition (PWA)
50 W. 17th St., 8th Fl., New York, NY 10011
(212) 647-1415 • (800) 828-3280 • fax: (212) 647-1419
The People with AIDS Coalition provides a hot line for AIDS treatment information and peer counseling for individuals with AIDS. The coalition publishes *PWA Newsline*, a monthly magazine containing treatment information, news analysis, and features on people living with AIDS; and *SIDAhora*, a Spanish/English quarterly concerned with AIDS in the Hispanic community.

Rockford Institute
934 N. Main St., Rockford, IL 61103
(815) 964-5053 • e-mail: rkfdinst@bossnt.com
The institute seeks to rebuild moral values and recover the traditional American family. It believes that AIDS is a symptom of the decline of the traditional family, and it insists that only by supporting traditional families and moral behavior will America rid itself of the disease. The institute publishes the periodicals *Family in America* and the *Religion & Society Report* as well as various syndicated newspaper articles that occasionally deal with the topic of AIDS.

Sex Information and Education Council of the United States (SIECUS)
130 W. 42nd St., Suite 350, New York, NY 10036
(212) 819-9770 • fax: (212) 819-9776
e-mail: siecus@aol.com • Internet: http://www.siecus.org
SIECUS is an organization of educators, physicians, social workers, and others who support the individual's right to acquire knowledge of sexuality and who encourage responsible sexual behavior. The council promotes comprehensive sex education for all children that includes AIDS education, teaching about homosexuality, and instruction about contraceptives and sexually transmitted diseases. Its publications include fact sheets, annotated bibliographies by topic, the booklet *Talk About Sex*, the bimonthly *SIECUS Report*, and the books *Winning the Battle: Developing Support for Sexuality and HIV/AIDS Education* and *How to Talk to Our Children About AIDS*.

BIBLIOGRAPHY OF BOOKS

Elinor Burkett — *The Gravest Show on Earth: America in the Age of AIDS.* Boston: Houghton Mifflin, 1995.

Alan Cantwell Jr. — *Queer Blood: The Secret AIDS Genocide Plot.* Los Angeles: Aries Rising Press, 1993.

Ralph J. DiClemente and John L. Peterson, eds. — *Preventing AIDS: Theories and Methods of Behavioral Interventions.* New York: Plenum, 1994.

Peter H. Duesberg — *Infectious AIDS: Stretching the Germ Theory Beyond Its Limits.* Berkeley, CA: North Atlantic Books, 1996.

Peter H. Duesberg — *Inventing the AIDS Virus.* Washington, DC: Regnery Publishing, 1996.

Bryan J. Ellison and Peter H. Duesberg — *Why We Will Never Win the War on AIDS.* El Cerrito, CA: Inside Story Communications, 1994.

Steven Epstein — *Impure Science: AIDS, Activism, and the Politics of Knowledge.* Berkeley: University of California Press, 1996.

M. Daniel Fernando — *AIDS and Intravenous Drug Use: The Influence of Morality, Politics, Social Science, and Race in the Making of a Tragedy.* Westport, CT: Praeger, 1993.

Michael Fumento — *The Myth of Heterosexual AIDS.* New York: Basic Books, 1990.

Nancy Goldstein and Jennifer L. Manlowe, eds. — *The Gender Politics of HIV/AIDS in Women: Perspectives on the Pandemic in the United States.* New York: New York University Press, 1997.

Robin Gorna — *Vamps, Virgins, and Victims: How Can Women Fight AIDS?* London: Cassell, 1996.

Lawrence O. Gostin and Zita Lazzarini — *Human Rights and Public Health in the AIDS Pandemic.* New York: Oxford University Press, 1997.

Christine Grady — *The Search for an AIDS Vaccine: Ethical Issues in the Development and Testing of a Preventive HIV Vaccine.* Bloomington: Indiana University Press, 1995.

Leonard G. Horowitz — *Emerging Viruses: AIDS and Ebola: Nature, Accident or Intentional?* Rockport, MA: Tetrahedron, 1996.

Earvin Johnson — *What You Can Do to Avoid AIDS.* New York: Times Books, 1996.

Jeffrey A. Kelly — *Changing HIV Risk Behavior: Practical Strategies.* New York: Guilford Publications, 1995.

Ann Kurth, ed. — *Until the Cure: Caring for Women with HIV.* New Haven, CT: Yale University Press, 1993.

Susan Moore, Doreen Rosenthal, and Anne Mitchell	*Youth, AIDS, and Sexually Transmitted Diseases*. New York: Routledge, 1997.
Jacques Normand, David Vlahov, and Lincoln E. Moses, eds.	*Preventing HIV Transmission: The Role of Sterile Needles and Bleach.* Washington, DC: National Academy Press, 1995.
Ann O'Leary	*Women at Risk: Issues in the Primary Prevention of AIDS.* New York: Plenum, 1995.
Cindy Patton	*Fatal Advice: How Safe-Sex Education Went Wrong.* Durham, NC: Duke University Press, 1996.
Cindy Patton	*Last Served? Gendering the HIV Pandemic.* Bristol, PA: Taylor & Francis, 1994.
Martin A. Plant	*AIDS, Drugs, and Prostitution.* New York: Routledge, 1993.
Josh Powell	*AIDS and HIV-Related Diseases: An Educational Guide for Professionals and the Public.* New York: Insight Books, 1996.
Gabriel Rotello	*Sexual Ecology: AIDS and the Destiny of Gay Men.* New York: Dutton, 1997.
William B. Rubenstein, Ruth Eisenberg, and Lawrence O. Gostin	*The Rights of People Who Are HIV Positive: The Authoritative ACLU Guide to the Rights of People Living with HIV Disease and AIDS.* Carbondale: Southern Illinois University Press, 1996.
Mary Kay Ryan and Arthur D. Shattuck	*Treating AIDS with Chinese Medicine.* Berkeley, CA: Pacific View Press, 1994.
Inon I. Schenker, Galia Sabar-Friedman, and Francisco S. Sy, eds.	*AIDS Education: Interventions in Multi-Cultural Societies.* New York: Plenum, 1997.
Mark S. Senak	*HIV, AIDS, and the Law: A Guide to Our Rights and Challenges.* New York: Insight Books, 1996.
Lorraine Sherr, Catherine Hankins, and Lydia Bennett, eds.	*AIDS as a Gender Issue: Psychosocial Perspectives.* Bristol, PA: Taylor & Francis, 1997.
Michelangelo Signorile	*Life Outside: The Signorile Report on Gay Men: Sex, Drugs, Muscles, and the Passages of Life.* New York: HarperCollins, 1997.
James Monroe Smith	*AIDS and Society.* Upper Saddle River, NJ: Prentice Hall, 1996.
Ben Sonder	*Epidemic of Silence: The Facts About Women and AIDS.* Danbury, CT: Franklin Watts, 1995.
Robert T. Trotter, ed.	*Multicultural AIDS Prevention Programs.* Binghamton, NY: Haworth Press, 1996.

Simon Watney

Policing Desire: Pornography, AIDS, and the Media. Minneapolis: University of Minnesota Press, 1997.

Robert E. Willner

Deadly Deception: The Proof that Sex and HIV Absolutely Do Not Cause AIDS. Boca Raton, FL: Peltec Publishing, 1994.

Qingcai Zhang and Hung-Yuan Hsu

AIDS and Chinese Medicine. Long Beach, CA: Oriental Healing Arts Institute, 1995.

INDEX

Acer, David, 72, 80
acupuncture
  disease-prevention aspects of, 188
  with herbal treatments, 184
  techniques, 185-86
Africa
  heterosexual HIV epidemic in, 29, 31
African Americans
  and violence due to HIV status, 69
  women, may fear mandatory testing, 54
AIDS
  effects on nutritional status, 177
  fears of
    are often irrational, 143-44
    must be faced, 83
  malnutrition associated with, 176
    risk-screening is needed, 178
  new cases in U.S., 30
  patients. See people with AIDS
  public health strategies have failed, 43
  risks to heterosexuals is low, 34
    con, 29, 44, 113
  stigma of, 94
  treatments for. See treatments for AIDS
  vaccine for, 31
  see also HIV
AIDS education
  cost evaluation of, 136-37
  discourages high-risk behavior, 133,
    135
  has had poor results, 139-40
  has modified high-risk behavior
    among gay men, 135
    con, 139-40
  impact evaluation is needed, 134
  misrepresentations of, 140-41
  peer-led, 136
  should address needs of gay
    community, 139-40
  should target high-risk groups, 146
AIDS Project Los Angeles, 133
Altman, Lawrence K., 20
American Civil Liberties Union
  (ACLU), 45, 50
American Dietetic Association, 175
American Journal of Medicine, 142
American Medical Association
  on contact notification, 91
American Psychological Association, 59
Americans with Disabilities Act of
  1990, 62
Ammann, Arthur J., 46, 47
Antiviral Therapy, 18
Aristotle, 77
Arizona

medical marijuana ballot measure in,
  167-68
  sends wrong message to children,
    170-71
Armentano, Paul, 167
Asia
  heterosexual HIV epidemic in, 29
Axelrod, David, 43
AZT (azidothymidine), 24, 25, 47,
  146, 152
  function of, 154
  HIV's resistance to, 19, 161
  integration into Chinese therapies, 187
  in prevention of newborn AIDS, 49,
    52, 58

Barr, Mike, 25, 160
Bayer, Ronald, 95, 107
Bennett, William, 48
Bergalis, Kimberly, 71, 73, 74
Berndtson, Keith, 76
blood lymphocytes, 30
  see also macrophages; T cells
blood supply
  testing of, 75
Brown, Marion, 68

California
  ballot initiatives in, 100-101
  HIV confidentiality laws in, 97
  medical marijuana ballot measure in,
    167-68, 170
    sends wrong message to children,
      170-71
Cameron, Paul, 112
Canadian Dietetic Association, 175
Centers for Disease Control and
  Prevention (CDC), 34, 44, 105
  on condom use among teens, 115
  on evaluation of AIDS education
    programs, 134
  on HIV testing, 47, 51, 68, 101
    of health care workers, 72
    of newborns, 51-52
    of pregnant women, 49
  overstates AIDS risk, 36
Ch'i Kung. See Qigong
Chinese therapies, in AIDS treatment
  acupuncture, 184, 185-86
    disease-prevention aspects of, 188
  herbs, 184-85
  integration with Western medicine,
    186-87
  relaxation techniques, 187-88
Chlebowski, R.T., 177